Jc ~~~~~~ Reluctant

Air Steward

Unique insights into the airline industry by a

male stewardess

SIMON J. MARTON

Still here? Good. Carry on…

Dedications

(It's nice to see your name in print)

With love and thanks to my beautiful wife, Helen, my family and friends like Gav, Bobby, Jason and Jammer for keeping me on my toes, and keeping me going. Gratitude and appreciation to Steph Boxall who proof-read my drafts with her keen eyes and editorial skills. With thanks to all those whom I have ever worked alongside, for your good humour, camaraderie and professionalism. With thanks especially to Jesus who has never let me go.

All photos contained taken by Simon J. Marton; copyright. *The front cover photo of a landing L1011 Tristar on runway 2-6 Left was taken by myself, as the evening sun went down at LGW sometime in the autumn of 1996, using a Canon IXUS APS camera with a 400 ISO film. The selfie is of me with Gav's safari Land Rover. The cap makes me feel so young, as Frank Sinatra once sang, although it's doubtful he was singing about a baseball cap.

I am a proud supporter of Action on Hearing Loss to raise awareness of how airline workers, drummers and other musicians could prevent damage to their hearing through exposure to loud music and amplified instruments.

ACTION ON HEARING LOSS
A national charity since 1911

As much as I love using their gear, the following two companies' products have been largely responsible for damaging my hearing. However, just like a cat that keeps coughing up hairballs, I never seem to learn, and still advocate them. (The drums and cymbals that is – not the hairballs.)

SONOR

Drumming's great, but the thing I've found out is that everyone loves the idea of a drummer until they live with one.

Foreword

Dear friend,

I'm a simple man in my late 40's, who likes the idea of owning a drinks cabinet and a wine cellar. My dad's Italian and my mum passed away about ten years ago. I have four children and it's as much as I can do to stay awake long enough with my wife to watch an episode of *EastEnders* on iPlayer at bedtime. I live just outside Bath, England and my main worries are financial, my family and how quickly life is zooming by. I'm ageing all right, and I can see it on the faces of my peers and heroes. I went body-boarding in Cornwall last summer at Perranporth Beach and was amazed at how many middle-aged (and older) men there were bobbing up and down among the younger ones, grinning and eagerly awaiting the next major wave to surge and violently propel us to the shore. I am not just a middle-aged man. I was younger once and at various points in my life, among other things, I was an air-steward.

I know we are interested in others' journeys and their defining events. The words I write are not necessarily wisdom-filled, but contain my slant, my insights and my perceptions as I make my journey. My caveat is that they are my honest observations and I don't have any intention of being political, nor slanderous. I don't claim to have had a more interesting or more privileged walk than yourself. Because I worked a while in the airline industry, I will use stories and anecdotes to get my points across. Sometimes, we feel as though we are in the departure lounge, filled with a prolonged sense of nervous expectation, while at other times, we are up in the air, gazing thoughtfully and in respectful wonder at panoramas in the skies. A lot of the time, however, I bet you feel like me – on autopilot.

At times I also felt like a foreigner in another world. I remember a time mid-flight on one of my first airlines, one of my female colleagues hoisted her leg in the air – and it was a fine leg – to adjust her tights. I didn't know where to look and realising, she said to me: "Oh, I'm sorry – I forgot, you're straight aren't you?!" I nodded, with a kind of Benny Hill smirk. Years later, a friend's teenage son asked me: "Simon, why do you always do women's jobs?" I recall snapping back: "I don't always do women's jobs!!" In reality, I was a reluctant air steward: a straight guy in another world, but pretty good at my job by all accounts. I went AWOL once and less than three months after the managers' meeting and an official letter of reprimand, they promoted me. Hardly the Midas touch, but perhaps deep down, they liked me.

You may be thinking, "Does the world need another expose of this sort?" You would be right – it doesn't, but that's not why I write. My first effort was on a completely different set of subjects which happened to incorporate my airline experiences, but I felt that the latter had to be chronicled separately. I still intend to write the book I want to which is on the subject of men, our identity and mental health.

In the meantime, may this book entertain you and perhaps even inspire you.

Simon Marton, June 2019.

Journey of a Reluctant Air-Steward

Contents

Preface (the bit you can skip...)

Everyone's trying to escape something....

I discovered this truth when my housemate, Baldy B and I happened to be on a winter's evening coach together travelling up to Heathrow (LHR) from Gatwick (LGW). Let's just say her nickname was her own lookout. She was off to catch a flight to see her ageing mum in Spain, while I was heading home via LHR central bus station. "Simon," she said, with an air of wisdom, "everyone who does this job is escaping something...."

For her, it was her old life in South Wales, a controlling ex-husband and mixed memories leading her to reinvent herself, find a new life and succeed in something she wanted. She certainly found her fit in the long-haul crew world, wearing her red uniform and black patent heels well with a twist of glamour in her swept-up hair – she was a kind of bottle-blonde *Memphis Belle* with down-to-earth humanity and a dirty chuckle. When she spoke of escape, it made me ponder things in my uncomfortable National Express seat all the way home. Maybe I was trying to escape something, or at least try something new which could lead me to find my path in life- wherever that may lead, and if it was in a succession of aeroplane journeys, then so be it. I told myself often that you never know what may happen if you keep yourself open to new experiences, and say 'yes' to opportunities as they come. 'Keep on moving' was the song Soul to Soul used to sing on the radio and it made sense to me; don't stop, you'll find yourself...

What was I escaping? The feeling that I had outgrown the city where I grew up, as lovely as it was there. The knowledge that I had no real prospects without a degree, and the desire to take the path not taken. I craved adventure and the unexpected, believing that an aircraft could take me into the unknown. In some ways I was right. You never knew who you might be working with, whom you might bump into, what conversations might lead you into something new....I would return home to see the folks usually every two weeks so I became a regular on National Express, becoming used to their idea of customer service and the 50/50 driver-mood. Sometimes if you were 'lucky', there might even be a hostess service, but it was unusual for me to have a coffee since badly burning the roof of my mouth the first time. The joys of machine-coffee served at 97 degrees. I would set off on the Gatwick Jet-link then change to the 403 service. Invariably I would end up waiting for a coach at LHR in the evenings and watch from my bench. "People-watching will never go out of fashion", as my mum used to say to me, who – funnily enough– worked in fashion. I used to watch other airport workers come and go, along with regular passengers, from families to solo travellers, all sorts of skin colours, ages, dress and baggage.

I was once taking a coach back from Gatwick to my hometown and found myself sitting next to an Australian guy in his mid thirties, a biker like me, and as we talked about off-roading

and his wife back home, I warmed to him because he was so easy
to talk to and had a rich array of stories related directly to his
talent. He was a didgeridoo player and it took him all around the
world. He spoke of a gig he had done a couple of weeks before,
performing in front of the king and queen of Sweden at their
'Festival of Water' in Stockholm. As he got off ahead of me, he
gave me a cassette: 'Native Ground' was its title, his collaboration
with guitar and percussion, and it made great chill-out music.
There was a man who obeyed something primal in him – his gift
and willingness to travel opened doors for him. I sometimes think
of him and where he might be now, because that brief encounter
taught me to be receptive to others for they can sometimes point
you in the right direction.

This idea of escape never left me, and when I returned to work, I
looked at my colleagues differently. There were girls and boys from
various counties as well as continents, and everyone had a story.
Mitch told me he was so full of metal plates from rally-car racing
accidents that he would often trigger the metal sensors at security,
and he also gave me some very good advice when I was tempted to
leave my first airline three months in: "Don't jump ship mid-
season- see it through." If I had followed my leanings, I would have
ended up joining a worse-performing airline, and seeing something
through felt right. I had learnt that from working with Yiannis in
Greece: his wife told me that I was the only person who had ever
managed to stick a whole six months working with him in the
kitchen. We could spend eight hours or more working silently

alongside each other, creating anything from Greek salads and Moussaka, to swordfish kebabs and Cordon Bleu steaks.

Life was pretty simple and carefree during that first summer season airline contract, and the only planning you had to do was make sure your roster was at hand, stay within earshot of the phone on standby duties and make sure your uniform was immaculate for a flying day. This was just before mobile phones became widespread and affordable, so you made your own fun rather than relying on a screen to entertain you. Music was my passion, but I had to lay my drums aside when I joined the airlines. That summer, 1996, I used to play my sticker-decorated acoustic guitar in the garden knocking out Lenny Kravitz and Crowded House tunes, hang out with friends I had made and go to work; simple. I smile as I write, because life now with dependants is very different – I'm older and perhaps a little more responsible.

This didn't all happen out of nowhere. If you are anything like me, you will look back at your life and see connection points, a little like a join-the-dots- game in a children's colouring book. In my early 20's, I had grown my dark hair long and curly, wore black almost-exclusively and was single-minded: I was only going to pursue music. I had confidence in that, owing to some band success, recordings, radio-play and national press, but not in my daily working abilities. When asked what I did, I told people I worked "in aviation". I actually worked as a cleaner in an air traffic control college ten minutes walk away from my folk's house, and shortly after this, I started to work out-front and in the wash-up at a friendly city-centre bistro. As I hit 24 years old, my sister who was working at the same restaurant as me announced that she was going to work on the Greek island of Santorini, and I was to come too. I resisted: *What if I miss something back here? What about my friends? What about music?* By the time I had committed myself to an open ticket to Athens with Virgin Atlantic (VS), it was too late to argue, and sometime in May 1995, I found myself on a night flight from LHR with my sister and an Irish friend of hers on a VS Airbus A320 – registration G-OUZO. Landing helplessly tired at 04.30, we spent the extra £50 each on an Olympic Airways direct commuter flight to Thira (JTR), which took 50 minutes, rather than endure ten hours on the ferry, which would have helpfully stopped at every other island in the Cyclades en route.

Working in Greece for a summer season gave me confidence in feeling able to root myself somewhere new and forge new friendships with people abroad. We were all on a similar journey together – international workers in different bars and restaurants who were unified by laughter, hard work and an unseen bond – a camaraderie that I guess would have been similar to those who were conscripted into national service. Another language emerged to identify people, sometimes by where they worked, e.g. *Jimmy Souvlaki* or *Yiannis Albatross*, and sometimes by the motorbike they rode, eg, *Mr Roulis Chopper, Stratos CR250*, or even *Jimmy Super Tenere*. Of course there were bound to be guys who were too cool, too aloof to be engaged in any conversation – often club owners on

Honda Transalp 600s. I knew who I could engage with and whom I should avoid, but for the most part I found my feet. I could leave my country and make friends thousands of miles away, be attracted to girls and sometimes attract them too, earn money seven days a week without a day off, and be my own man living a simple life in the sun. I think an experience such as this can only be recommended. I also discovered 'a new me': motorbikes, Amstel beer and a deep suntan. I felt cool, learned how to handle a DT200 and occasionally, even wore colours.

I returned to England in late '95 and because of the nature of living on an island, however idyllic it sounds, there isn't much variety. Within a week of being back in the UK, I had done more than I had done in six months away. My friends collected me from Heathrow in a limo, I took the first part of my motorbike test, had a flying lesson in a Cessna 152 and saw The Wildhearts at Bristol University where I was kicked in the face (amazing gig)…. Something more had happened to me while I was in Greece, and it could have been anywhere, but I realised that for a lot of my co-workers – boys and girls – this was just one in a sequence of away-from-home experiences. They had all been saving up cash for the next instalment: some were off to the Far East, India and Australia, others to the States, others to continue around Europe, but the common theme was a goal – continuous movement. I had treated this as a one-off mini-adventure with the safety net that I was only four hours direct-flight-time from home. Triple the travel time at least, if I took a ferry and then a flight from Athens.

This experience away from home, finding friends and being able to uproot and adapt quickly meant that my next phase was going to be obvious. A friendly waiter in a restaurant, with a childhood love of aeroplanes and a willingness to travel would probably make an excellent air steward....

Chapter One

"Stand back – I am fully trained!"

All my young life, I was besotted by aeroplanes. If something went over above, I *had to know what it was*. One day, aged 14, I even punched my hand through my bedroom window in eagerness to identify a passing jetliner. I even used to recreate engine noises with my mouth, which the cool kids at school would ask me to do before walking off laughing in disbelief, but I couldn't help myself. Those feelings switched to making music in my teens, but these two passions remain as strong now as they did back then.

Somewhere along the way, for such a seemingly confident person, I lacked self-belief, and I am sure, dear reader, that I am not alone in that. When I was about 12, I was returning from a holiday in Portugal with my family. Why my mum insisted on me looking 'smart' in an M&S velour sweatshirt, I'll never know. It was probably more for her to impress the captain, just in case I visited the flight-deck, which was usually the highlight of any holiday. My folks got talking to the chief steward onboard the British Airtours Tristar G-BEAM (aka *Silver Jubilee Rose*). A couple had been complaining about a little four-year old girl who had been running up and down the aisles playing. Her noise was upsetting them. The No.1 explained: "What they – nor the little girl know – is that her parents died on holiday in a car crash and we're carrying their coffins home in the cargo hold." All I could think of was how that little girl's life was going to change forever.

In a very different way, mine was to change too…. Fast forward to just under thirty years later and I found myself standing next to Terry, one of my crew members outside the entrance to Hartsfield-Jackson Atlanta International Airport (ATL). We were waiting for the crew bus to come pick all 14 of us up, when the distant earth-shuddering roar of a departing liner could be heard penetrating the warm evening sundown. Terry looked wistful for a second as he announced, "I'll never get bored of that sound…". I knew exactly what he meant – that sound has become almost as important as my heartbeat, and as loud as my tinnitus. The latter was brought on by my stubborn refusal to wear ear plugs in my band days. (I was too young and too rock 'n' roll apparently.) When I got married, my two housemates bought me a scrapped wing section off an old Dan-Air 727, an aileron I think, and it was large enough to dominate the reception entrance on a wooden stand, so that guests could write their well-wishing messages on it. Two messages stood out: "I told you he wasn't gay" and "The flying'll never leave your blood, Sime…".

One Tuesday evening in the restaurant about eleven years previously, the chef's grill had caught fire, but neither he nor my boss could put it out. The fire brigade were called. This was to be my chance to shine, as I had kept it under wraps that I had completed an aircraft-fire-fighting course with Bristol Airport's

Firefighters the previous week, in preparation for a new career. I was to utter the words I had always wanted to emit. I turned to my boss, who had his cravat over his mouth, tears streaming from the smoke, and commanded assertively: "Stand back, Dick – I'm fully trained!" Carefully choosing a CO_2 fire extinguisher, I pulled out the pin, squeezed the handle to test and rushed in low to tackle the base of the flames and upwards, discharging the whole container. I had adhered to my training and emerged triumphant. What I didn't know was that because a window had been left open – invisible through the smoke – the fire had reignited, so whilst it was commendable that I had used carbon dioxide, the triangle of fire remained intact. (I had considered the dry powder extinguisher but didn't want to make a mess.) Unfortunately, there was much more of a mess left behind, as by the time the fire was under control of the experts, it had burnt through a staircase in the flats above, and had forced closure of the restaurant for ten days to allow time for repairs. So much for training – I had managed to assist a fire rather than extinguish it.

A few months later I would be in the aircraft galley mock-up at the Caledonian hangar, Airport Perimeter road, Gatwick, running through the firefighting drill for an oven fire at 37,000ft, being watched by giggling girls and boys as I paced up and down like Percy from *Blackadder* in white overalls, desperately pulling circuit breakers and switches in the wrong order. But first, a haircut if I was going to do this properly. I thought I would cry at this loss, as my musician's identity had been wrapped up in my distinctive locks, which made me look like a cross between Andre Agassi '92 whenever I wore a white baseball cap, and Marc Bolan of T-Rex. Once back on my Honda MTX, I could nearly spin my Shoei helmet right round my head. Man, I must have wanted this change badly....

The start of applications and rejections

I sought counsel from a good friend's dad who had been high up in the MOD, as I received my first handful of applications forms, with details and answers carefully composed, then completed in pencil for the first edits. Biros and crossings-out don't do an applicant any favours, and are immediately discarded in favour of well-presented, easy-to-read pages, with succinct and to-the-point answers. My friend had just become a new-entrant fire-fighter in Brighton, so he was an obvious reference point. The list of British airlines I applied to between November 1995 and February 1996 included: British Airways (BA), Airtours, Air 2000, Monarch, Caledonian Airways, Goldcrest and Brymon.

I ended up being invited to interviews with Airtours, Brymon and BA. The first one saw me having to be on my best behaviour. It was in a Bristol hotel which my friend Gavin drove me to, and the two interviewers might as well have been Freddie Mercury-impersonators sporting bright blue *Butlins* jackets. Looking at the twelve of us, Freddie No.1 declared, "Any questions?" One of the girl candidates innocently asked, "Is there a first class on Airtours?" Quickly, Freddie No.1 replied smiling with his moustache slightly quivering: "It's all first class!" I desperately wanted to hum *We are the Champions*, but as much as this would have scored me ten points on the sarcasm scale, it would have soured my already-limited chances of success. They admitted they only had two places to fill (for a six month summer contract, which is how these charter airlines function), and it was always going to be the two girls who had travelled the furthest through the night who were going to land these positions. My "thanks, but no thanks" communication came through predictably within a few days.

The Brymon selection day lasted from 10.00 until 16.00. Brymon were a regional airline based out of Plymouth, with a larger base at Bristol, and operated as 'British Airways Express', being a wholly-owned subsidiary of 'the world's most tolerated airline' (as a well-travelled friend of mine once put it.) I was interviewed twice during the latter part of the day, but it was the first part of the day that was to be my forte. The organisers placed us around a table, in a hotel meeting room and whilst we introduced ourselves to each other, two smart-looking girls observed us, writing things down on their clipboards – possibly private shopping lists or even hate mail to be sent off later – we would never know.

When it came to introductions to the organisers, each of the ten of us was asked to give our name and say whom we had been talking to. Without fail, my name was mentioned every time, to which the comment came, "You seem to be popular, Simon…" Stage by stage, I seemed to be progressed through the day, even managing to say something during the first interview about disappearing into an aircraft toilet and coming out smiling: a nervous throwaway comment, which managed to make the blonde clip-boarders either side of the main interviewer collapse with laughter. The interviewer terminated the proceedings, and decided it was a signal to put me through to the final one. During the last one, the two ladies who were questioning me were quite different – older and humourless. The sort you might imagine working for the Department of Work and Pensions in senior management positions, awaiting retirement as the highlight of their lives. I recall a strange question: 'Simon, if you were a musical instrument what would you be?' My answer: "A classical guitar being played on a mountain." Another letter to add to my collection came within three working days.

The BA selection day came in March 1996 again at a prominent hotel, this time on the Bath Road, Hounslow and I could not believe just how many applicants were present, arriving in a steady stream all day no doubt. In the presentation we were given, we sat down to talks by various managers, working crew/ selectors, and I estimated two hundred or more candidates in that sitting alone. The recruitment phases were for BA 'Mid-fleet' which was a kind of hybrid set-up of short haul and long haul routes. (That fleet disappeared within a few years, and was to be reinvented nearly 15 years later for mainly accountancy reasons as you will see later on....)

As soon as I arrived, I was conscious of tall ladies and the odd gentleman, all besuited with clipboards, watching my every move. As soon as I sat down, made any kind of slight move or adjusted my tie, it was noted rapidly as I became aware of a pen moving in my peripheral vision. The morning involved various mathematical and academic reasoning tests, but I fell to pieces at an 'introduce yourself to the group' stage, as when it came to my turn, I entirely forgot what the two candidates whom I had been talking to actually did. I swear I saw Freddie No.1 and Freddie No. 2 there, but maybe I was seeing things. I didn't see any 'fat-bottomed girls' there either.

The rejection letters from Monarch and BA came through before any hint of an actual interview, but in the meantime I took a one-day cabin crew preparation course at a hotel in LGW to aid my chances of being selected. One thing made me stand out. When the twenty five of us were individually asked to make a presentation about the person next to us, the girl next to me announced that in stark contrast to all the girls who "would like to be on a beach sunbathing", "Simon would like to appear in a Daffy Duck cartoon…" The course presenter seemed to like this, as apparently it made me memorable. She also said I didn't know what to do with my hands, but felt she was nit-picking and apart from that, it was excellent. My heart nearly burst and I became aware of slightly jealous looks from pretty girls, who were probably thinking they should have plumped for being Daffy or Elmer Fudd instead of sunning themselves. This was to be the best £80 I had spent at the time, as the next airline I went for....

Selected....

It was a beautiful early-summer's day morning at LGW in April 1996, and as I walked along the Perimeter Road from the South Terminal, I took in the engine sounds from behind the hedges where I imagined airliners from all sorts of countries engaging in their activities. I stopped for moment as I heard an approaching whine increasing in volume, but nothing could prepare me for the sudden looming of a low-climbing 747 'classic' in Virgin Atlantic colours right over my head, strikingly white and red against the clear blue skies of West Sussex. I watched it slowly ascend into the distance, marvelling at the spectacle, and thought to myself, "Is this Heaven....?" Within ten minutes I arrived at 'Caledonian House', near the BA Engineering base. The selection morning lasted about two hours, as we were processed, weighed and dispatched into a medium-sized waiting room. Several of us were called out to leave the bulk of the boys and girls behind. Chaperoned into a smaller room, I resigned myself to believe that this was another chapter in the catalogue of near-misses, and that I was never to make the grade. The interviewer had better news to announce: we had been taken out of that room, as *we* had been the successful ones and were to be taken to the interview.

It was still in the balance for a week following, and the tensely-awaited A4 envelope containing my offer of employment and contract arrived in the post on a Saturday morning. I opened it in my parent's bedroom, and one by one, we all cried. I think the dog even cried too. I would like to think that even the postman, the car mechanic and the newsagent from down the road were also in tears, though I think this may be pushing the point a little too hard. I had been spared from wearing an Airtours blue blazer and narrowly missed Caledonian tartan, but Goldcrest were a part of the latter's organisation and I had finally made it – within six short months of leaving Greece, I was in.

The training course offered by Caledonian Airways was a little like the Virgin Atlantic stickers I had begged for, when I was charged 15,000 Drachma by the airline for not getting my ticket stamped in Syntagma Square, Athens – "You'll never forget your first time." The two senior cabin crew trainers, Katie and Moira, assured us: "This training will set you up for life…". Three weeks packed with more information than I felt I could handle on the L1011 Tristar, exams, security passes and another haircut, before which, I said to Des (the resident hairdresser and fellow biker): "Just don't give me a pinhead air steward haircut!" He was gracious enough to absorb my unintended rudeness, with a quip: "Oh, I just let the clippers do their job…!" and I apologised for my outburst. Des was to be a great agony aunt in the following three years. I was now a trained-up cabin crew member at last, or C/A (cabin attendant), and brushed up quite well in uniform.

They let me loose on a Saturday afternoon supernumerary (observation) flight to FAO (Faro, Portugal) with classroom mates

Tina and Trotter. I liked the atmosphere on-board, the mix of characters, the speed of the routines and even clearing-in, feeling it was a job I could enjoy. The two stand-out features of that flight were that the captain fed back the football results to the cabin to an eruption of cheers from some of the passengers (aka *pax*), and during short-finals into FAO as the giant Tristar flared, all of a sudden hairy arms went into action pushing the three throttle levers forwards as a voice confirmed with authority: "The LTU's still on the runway…!" A German wide-body 767 had yet to vacate Faro's sole (short) runway and we aborted the landing, initiating what is known in the trade as a 'go-around' to avoid the possibility of a collision on landing. Five of us were in the flight-deck at the time, and I was to work with the First Officer's (F/O) wife at a future company: it's a small (airline) world.

On the same trip, Tina had asked two camp guys Eduardo and Miguel what they thought of me. One replied flatly, "Not my type." He was too busy checking out the well-built cleaner's arms as he vacuumed the seats pre-departure. The other looked me up and down and gave his wordless verdict in an approving tone: "Mmmm…!" Oh no….. I noted that I was a rare breed: I was in the *SAS- (Straight Air-Stewards)* and was always to be outnumbered by gay guys who dominate this profession. Every so often I might have my bum pinched or my shirt and tie straightened for me, but I figured it was a sign that I was liked. Thankfully, that's as far as the 'liking' went.

Once on-line, I could forget most of the training and concentrate on the job in hand: to be the charter airline comedian. My main rival for the trophy was Rob with his dry Northern wit. When the 13 of us were asked during one of Tina's pre-flight briefings for any language skills on a Malaga, he replied dourly, "Yes: Serbo-Croat and Swahili." In fairness, you never know who might need those skills.

Tristars – what lies beneath....

The L1011 Tristar, despite looking comedic with its cheeky dolphin-nose, had been ahead of its time when launched in the Seventies. The DC-10 was the only other wide-bodied tri-jet and was its main rival. The L1011 was an aircraft built by Lockheed, who usually built high-performing secret military projects like the SR-71A and the world-leading 'Space-Shuttle'. It was a great aircraft to work on as unlike many other boring tubes, it had so many hiding places, including a UFG (underfloor galley) which you accessed by a pair of slimline lifts. Why, oh why, was it always when I tried to go downstairs mid-flight, that some joker would trap me between the levels by operating the toggle switches at cabin level to override mine while the senior's back was turned? I guess they knew I could take it. There were also a pair of UFG escape hatches incorporated too just in case of electrical failure. I think it was on a Malaga (AGP), that Amber (peroxide blonde bob) emerged from one of these, to get a right mouthful from the senior, Gina (dark bob) on the dangers of being crushed by the lift. I think she burst into tears – something to do with not having had any sleep the night before and not wanting to snore in front of her new boyfriend…. Another time, en route to TFS (Tenerife Sud), I called down to Dawn (no bob) who was galley lead working alone downstairs, in my best deep guttural voice which suddenly demanded through her speaker: "Dawn! Dawn! I need Coca Cola….!" Yes, sure the 20 cans arrived a couple of minutes later, but with the explanation that she had screamed and dropped a whole tray of 'minerals' (cans), as the voice had sounded demonic; what hadn't helped was that she had been reading 'Memonech' (sequel to a vampire trilogy) at the time, plus a decompression panel was missing in the UFG exposing a dark chasm in the chamber beyond…. Ah, the UFG – such simple fun.

I do know from research that a whole lot more sordid things happened on other airlines using the Tristar, but it's not really for here. People's sordid exploits are for readers of *The Mirror* and *The Sun,* and I would like to think I'm a little more upmarket – hold on a second – I need the loo. That's better. We had, I think, a row of seven toilets at the rear, and on a Dalaman, Turkey (DLM), it was my job to check the lavatories for re-stocking and signs of hijack warnings (messages) as an extreme. In comical mode, having seen at the end of the flight that someone had blocked a lavatory, I announced to my colleagues as we were awaiting the crew bus in the sun: "Someone's left a message in the toilet." They all replied earnestly: "What did it say?" I offered: "Should I put it in the log-book?" Only the pilots sniggered.

Talking of hijacks, the training course made you aware of *Stockholm Syndrome*, so named after the infamous 1973 Swedish bank robbery: should you ever be unlucky enough to be hijacked on a plane and end up long enough in the company of those who took you and your fellow pax against your collective will, then this phrase describes what could happen to those who then align themselves with the hijackers' objectives and core beliefs. The only thing I knew about Sweden was that it had a high proportion of blonde-haired perfectly featured persons, and nearly everyone has heard of IKEA. As regards *Stockholm Syndrome*, the only affiliation I had ever felt for anyone trying to make me doing something against my will, was my mum making me eat peas as a child. I always came around to her way of thinking.

You soon found out that when you hand drinks in plastic cups to the pilots you do it outboard of the controls – to the extreme left of the captain and extreme right of the F/O to avoid spillage over the sensitive main console area containing radio equipment. Coffee over those at 35,000ft and you have a little problem – no communication with the ground. It did actually happen to me on a T/A (turnaround) in the Netherlands, when the F/O stretched his arms just at the moment I entered the tiny ATR flight-deck, sending a 'tea-white plus one (sugar)' over the radio console and switches. This would have grounded the aircraft 500 miles from home, causing significant disruption. To Capt. Maunder's delight, I rapidly returned with a load of blue roll and hurriedly addressed the spillage: "Good mopping, Simon!" My heart swelled. Maybe all those days as a cleaner weren't wasted after all.

There is an on-board hierarchy known as the 'chain of command' and relates largely to location. It starts with the captain, then the F/O who understandably control the ship and issue ultimate authority. Then, outside of the flight deck (F/D) the SCCM/ No.1 (Senior cabin crew member) in the cabin is the third in command, in charge of the cabin crew. The next in line is the No.2 or Purser depending on the size of the aircraft. The Purser could be the SCCM on a smaller aircraft. Juniors have various numbers allocated to them, usually relating to door-manning positions. Typically, one C/A is responsible for a maximum of fifty pax, according to CAA safety recommendations in the UK. As I understand it, this is broadly similar for most countries. There is one standard cabin announcement that the crew are trained for which no-one really wants to hear during the course of a routine flight. It will be a call for the SCCM to go the F/D. In all my flying days, it never happened, but should you hear it you'll know that something is definitely up....

Often the hardest things to cope with in those early Tristar days were the poorly regulated air-con, meaning it was incredibly warm for both us and pax, the lengthy delays during the summer as one late inbound impacted the next departure, and trying to stay awake on night-flights, sitting on metal bar-boxes in galleys, chatting or reading while pax were asleep. The average delay was seven hours. At the height of the holiday season, the aircraft was expected to perform two to three rotations (there-and-back journeys) per day, with little room for anything to go wrong. I was to discover that there are many things which could go wrong, from stray pax delaying a flight, missed air traffic control (ATC) slots, fights inside the terminal, technical faults and impromptu engineering checks. One day we had even been delayed for 26 hours, during which the pax had been given hotel accommodation (HOTAC). On the day of actual departure, a BA engineer walked through the cabin with the longest screwdriver I had ever seen. *Snap-on* would have been proud. It must have been almost a metre long, and swinging it as he walked through the forward cabin, in front of about one hundred and twenty pax sat waiting to go, he called out loudly to an unseen colleague, "It's alright Reg – I've fixed it!" We would never know quite what he had fixed, nor what Reg looked like, but I giggled in the mid-galley trying to imagine what on earth the pax might be thinking. ("Twenty six hours later and *that* screwdriver fixed the plane?!")

The aircraft needed a little more TLC than most, much like your elderly relative in the retirement home who still has all her faculties. Yet the Tristar had character and a certain charm despite its apparent unreliability. There were stubby metal cylinders with a retracting handle at doorway floor-points all along the plane, called 'mushrooms', which were anchor points for securing double-trolleys in the cabin. They were, if left up and unattended, also trip-hazards, especially for unsuspecting old ladies who weren't looking where they were going. Yes, the 70 year-old went flying after I had forgotten to push it back into the floor, and it would be the exact time when the base-manager was line-checking me. The victim was gracious enough not to punch my lights out, and the line-appraisal mentioned something like "always be careful with your mushrooms" which could have been good advice on so many levels....

Remember your training

As cabin crew members we are trained for many eventualities, so behind the smiles, designer uniforms, the elegance, and tea and coffee, there are more purposeful dynamics going on – a readiness for response to danger. The most likely moments for disaster are in the take-off and landing phases, so there are even 'SEATS' drills to go through in your head at those times. More recently, my cohort of customer service managers were undergoing safety and emergency procedures (SEP) training at BA's training headquarters, Cranebank, LHR. There were about 40 of us: a mix of pilots and cabin crew being prepped in a classroom for the big exercise of the day – how to react in an unplanned emergency landing. Funny how all the more-experienced flyers didn't respond to the invite to be the senior-in-charge for the exercise, so I stuck my paw in the air with nothing to lose and no face to save.

Even though you know these are simulations and the cabins are mock-ups, surprisingly you are still caught up in the decisions and related emotions, and you have to treat them as the real thing with the odd unexpected twist of events thrown at you by the watching instructors. (Apparently I did well, more or less a textbook effort.) When Renald and myself were later enacting the door-opening drill with power-assist failure, I couldn't understand the chuckles as the heavy Boeing 777 door hit the side of the cabin mock-up exterior. Apparently his assistance to push open the 80 kg door was unnecessary, as my pure adrenaline had enabled me to do what no-one else could manage alone. Maybe it was something to do with being used to pushing all those big motorbikes I've had, when they refused to start.

Following a chat with an F/O colleague about the limited chances of survival in a ditching scenario, I privately decided to reduce my use of such questions in pre-flight briefings. I remember groaning inwardly as I overheard a well-known male senior's voice buoyantly announce to his crew as I passed his table: "Okay, let's go through the ditching drill together…". There was nothing buoyant about the ditching drill. (Ahem.) I imagined the team's inward anxiety at being forced to repeat the long-winded drill ad verbatim for fear of being offloaded. Think about it: how many successful ditching attempts have there ever been, aside from the A320 on the Hudson River, NYC, or the 737-800 in New Guinea? (OK, conceded maybe it works sometimes….) There are several key SEP drills: Firefighting, Planned emergency landing, Unplanned emergency landing, Decompression and Ditching. Secondary drills include Rapid disembarkation, Hijacking procedures, Survival and so on. The slide raft drill was little bit of fun as it involved pulling each other out of the water. There's even a procedure for placing a suspected bomb in a 'least- risk location' which is usually near the tail area. You get used to a whole new language with references to 'BCF' (short for a chemical type of fire extinguisher), 'the rubber jungle' (appearance of yellow oxygen masks from overhead panels if the aircraft suffers a decompression) and 'the alert signal' (a phrase everyone dreads, which only the cabin crew would understand if given over the PA by the pilots). The fire-fighting, decompression, emergency landing and ditching drills are involved, thorough and a touch surreal when you are playing them out at Cranebank, yet the drills save lives.

I had been out of the airlines for a few years, when one afternoon in Morrisons, my heart rate increased rapidly when I saw the newspaper headlines and a photo of a familiar logo. I admit that I cried when I watched the TV footage of a well-executed BA777 evacuation on the runway at McCarrack International, Las Vegas, (LAS) following an engine fire and aborted take-off. *"It could've been me..."* was my first reaction. The commentary revealed that the crew did it as they were trained to, with every assertive command, redirection to alternative escape routes, slide deployment and door-guarding until inflation, evacuating all pax – and then themselves – after finally checking the cabin was completely empty. This training through five UK airlines has stayed with me and keeps me inwardly alert to the possibilities of danger everywhere, even from my cats, the toaster and the washing machine. (To date, it's even helped me take charge of road traffic accidents if I am first on the scene.) The nearest comparison I can draw is with the military, though my limited experience is confined to RAF cadets and the occasional night exercise on Salisbury Plain, Wiltshire, hearing stories from a relative who used to be a squaddie, and a liking for *Bad Lads' Army* on Channel Five.

I once found an abandoned carrier bag containing a car battery and some wire outside a Ford dealership on a busy Saturday afternoon in the fall of 2000. (Me and my band mates were trying to source some material from the drapers next door for a backdrop for our live shows. You see, a good backdrop works well with lighting effects, strobes and smoke machines.) Key components for bombs: Remember your training – detonator, fuse, timer and explosive. The salesman, midway through a deal, was politely dismissive- maybe he thought terrorist acts happen somewhere else, not in a world-heritage tourist city. I nearly offered him a crash-course in IED-recognition (Improvised Explosive Device), but he would have surely blown his sale of that new Ford Kuga. It turned out not to be a bomb, but belonged to some Chinese students who happened to like carrying old car batteries around town at weekends. They could have been considering opening an Oriental scrapyard, now there's a business idea.

It wasn't just safety we were trained in but AVMED (Aviation Medicine) or 'airline first aid'. Everything from CPR, cardiac arrest, angina and strokes, to concussion and compression, diabetes, epilepsy, and burns through to good old fashioned severed arteries and childbirth. There were ways you could use credit cards and parcel tape to stem the flow of blood when dealing with wounds. I disliked any talk of blood as it reminded me of when I had fainted in hospital when they took my blood pressure. (I had cracked my head open on a low beam, whilst excitedly leaping through the restaurant, and had to have stitches.) When I came around, I realised I had a worse injury from hitting my face on the side of a nearby wheelchair. My passport photo displayed these war-wounds. Another time, I was standing at the rear door of the ATR turboprop as the No.1 (senior crew member) taking a couple of minutes pre-boarding to watch airliners take off. My No.2 was checking safety equipment inside the cabin. "Life is great- I'm a No.1!", I said to myself before turning around too quickly, forgetting to duck slightly, and then cutting my forehead open on the metal door-sill. As I prepared to take the aircraft to LBA (Leeds Bradford) later on that evening as sole crew member, I personally went up to the seven pax onboard and explained that I hadn't been in a fight and I was quite safe to fly with. They smiled, albeit nervously. I am just over six foot tall, but quite personable.

So, fully trained, working for my first airline, I believed I could take on the world. Wrong of course. I have found that most of my training has been forgotten along the way and that most situations are a mixture of choosing your responses and 'blagging it.' Looking back that could sum up my career to date. This was to be the start of a random kind of journey, so cabin crew, get strapped into your jump seats, there go the double seat belt chimes....

Chapter Two

Pushback

This is the moment when you know you're actually going – backwards anyway – and you can be forgiven for the slightly nervous feeling in your stomach. Seat belt securely fastened and with no wish to draw attention to yourself by screaming "I want to get off!", you are committed to flying. It takes on average another 10 to 15 minutes to get to the runway holding point and follow the lines of departing traffic, listening to the whooshes and roars of accelerating jets on their take-off runs. Your turn soon.

While you sit in your seat gazing out of the window, the pilots are behind a bolted door taxi-ing slowly while completing pre-take off checks, maintaining radio contact with the tower and talking about performance cars, the football results or how attractive that girl is working at the back. The cabin crew are probably finishing off a coffee that was left on the galley worktop before the demo, making a last-minute toilet visit, checking oven electrics are off, securing latches and altering cabin lighting. They pass the cabin-secure check to the flight-deck and then get seated themselves in readiness for the departure, once they've put *OK!* magazine away or finished texting their boyfriend. I remember once forgetting to turn my phone off before T/O (take-off) and just managing to reply to a text to my wife to let her know the car keys she couldn't find were in my jeans upstairs in our bedroom, seconds before we thundered down the runway departing for PRG (Prague). If I hadn't replied, her day would have been ruined and as a consequence, mine too.

More OUZO?

Owing to a window in time, and knowing I would not have any leave to play with for another six months, I decided to nip over to Santorini for a quick four-day trip to surprise my sister just before I started my first training course. I had left a note on my pillow for my mum to tell her that by the time she read it, I would be checked in at London for a flight to Athens, and sorry for the waste of the mug of tea she had left me. As it happens she was marginally more upset over making me a cup of tea that I wasn't there to drink. When I got to LGW to catch G-OUZO again on the morning flight, it had been cancelled. Too much Ouzo the night before, I expect. Because I spoke nicely to the Virgin Atlantic (VS) lady with a radio, and happened to mention cunningly that I was soon to be in the trade, she immediately rebooked me onto an Olympic Airways (OA) flight out of LHR leaving in three hours, along with coach travel there, ahead of everyone else who was shouting abuse at the carrier's staff. At LHR, Aer Lingus were handling the boarding and watching Greeks at the departure gate was an education. The older women tended to have dyed blonde or gothic-red hair supported into style by ostentatious designer shades, and carried multiples of bags advertising luxury brands to display their status. No-one had any regard for a queue. I could see the pain on the faces of the gate-staff as the throng surged forward when the boarding was announced.

Once in the air, I watched proceedings while drinking a can of Mythos, until I fell asleep. Later on, I wandered down to the toilet and on return stopped to chat to one of the stewards in the rear A300 galley. He had dark collar-length curly hair, a thick moustache and was leaning his foot against a bar trolley handle, smoking a Marlboro Light. I dared to ask him: "Do you like your job?" He simply nodded silently, continuing to draw upon his lighted stick. I announced with the eagerness of a puppy trying to please his master, "I'm going to be cabin crew too next week!" Without looking at me, he simply nodded slowly again and I left him to it, understanding that he wanted to be left alone to draw comfort from his fag-break and possibly didn't like puppies. I watched the crew a while longer and on subsequent flights I took with OA. Some of the cabin staff were relics from years of nationalisation – much like British Rail or British Airways before being privatised, they could enjoy state money and perks without much interference, so the idea of 'service' was limited. Some were great, and that's a reflection across all airlines: what you experience as a traveller on the day really is inconsistent. From what I saw, passengers were often an inconvenience to be tolerated, and the cabins themselves were dated and worn. If you think that's harsh, check out some of the opinion websites and you'll laugh at the experiences many have had with this airline. The food generally though, was great in ECY (Economy) and the planes were well-flown by many ex-Hellenic Air Force pilots. For me, Olympic weren't bad, just funny.

In subsequent years I would use my staff travel perks to take my folks away on a couple of trips. (Parents can actually be fun to travel with, as you realise once you're in your mid-twenties plus, they aren't just Mum and Dad, but they have characters.) On one trip to see my sister, we landed at the old Athens airport (Hellenikon), and walked over to the domestic terminal – a well-worn building which resembled a local government office stuck in 1970. My mum went to enquire about some tickets, hoping to score us firm seats on the last evening flight to JTR. The OA agent, a balding man in his fifties, barely looked up at her, as he continued drawing on his cigarette whilst examining his pool coupons. When she asked him if there was any availability on the next flight, he took a drag on his fag and shrugging his shoulders, looked up at my mum and announced: "Maybe yes…maybe no." How helpful. She asked if he would take a look, so he tapped away in Morse code at an unseen keyboard, put down his lighted stick for a moment and bluntly stated: "Is full." It transpired that most transactions were like this. A plane could leave half-full on this basis, as it would depend on whether the ticketing agents were up for doing their jobs in that moment, or not. They seemed to be better at issuing penalties for ticket-changes. Even BAs Speed-wing consultancy had to rescue Olympic with a strategic direction and new business plan in 2000-2001 but it was little too late for many. Aegean stepped in with a slicker operation.

I made it back to England after my trip in time to start with Caledonian Airways on the Monday morning, but not before missing my return flight owing to a late ferry, followed by my taxi driver in Athens deciding to make a detour with two other persons first. As I arrived at the airport, I saw G-OUZO climbing into Greek airspace, leaving me to make a panic-call to my travel agent in the UK, to beg for a rebooking for the following morning. That was another 12 hours trying to sleep in a rigid airport seat while maintaining an eye on my bags all night.

Routines

Like any job, the feeling of reinventing the wheel sets in daily, but you have to fight it.

Routines are vital to keep the ship running smoothly. Waking up, washing-up, making breakfast, showering, getting changed and ready for work, instructing the children, finding your keys/badge/ID/bag, calling for the children to hurry up, breaking up a fight, shouting in frustration, leaving the house, locking the door, jumping in the car, forgetting something vital and then finally departing, saving the lecture for the car. That's a typical weekday routine in my home – just for *starting* the day.

Here's a typical routine for air cabin crew, once you've arrived at the airport, parked up and made it to the crew office/report centre….. Fumbling about for your pass, you swipe it and present it at the door, which should hopefully unlock and let you into another world: a world of wall-to-wall uniforms, which can be intimidating, where everyone seems to be watching each other out of the corners of their eyes. If you've ever wondered what an airline crew room looks like, it's like being in a busy railway station with immaculately uniformed boys and often glamorous-looking girls with swept-up hair coming and going or just waiting for a briefing or a friend, or simply reading a magazine while on airport standby. There are smiles and near-kisses on cheeks – the sort only women can manage without rubbing off their foundation, handshakes between middle-aged men with four gold stripes on their jacket-cuffs and youthful looking males with two or three gold bands on their sleeves, carrying black leather pilot's cases containing headsets and sandwiches, and acknowledging-looks from colleagues you recognise from three flights ago. At 06:00 on any given day, the crew report office is usually a hive of activity, especially for a charter airline, with boys and girls arriving in from night-flights as others are waiting to leave, in order to cross through security and either walk to the gates, or catch a 'crew-bus' to drive around the airfield to meet the aircraft on its stand. There are black wheelie bags presenting trip-hazards everywhere, each proudly displaying a 'CREW' tag, which is half for identifying the bag quickly, and the other half to draw attention to the owner's affiliation to a club that the public would probably like to know more about.

The cabin crew briefing is the stage where nerves can send your own heartbeat privately racing. What's the Senior (SCCM) like? That will be the question that will be burning for most junior new members. Are the SEP questions going to be difficult? Will I be offloaded (for lack of knowledge)? Is it going to be a hard day? I had found that the trick was to appear unfazed, as all air crew have been trained to the same knowledge levels, and it's just a case of knowing the drills sufficiently to repeat them back without even thinking about it. In real life, you would switch them on as quickly as you would open an email on your phone. Once you leave the briefing the rest is a well-executed blur of duties chronicled below.

The usual procedures

Arrive at aircraft (which should hopefully be empty of any airport personnel, cleaners, caterers,), stow crew-bags, prep cabin and galleys, safety (SEP) equipment and security checks, just enough time for a quick coffee and a chat with the dispatcher/turn-around manager, thumbs up to the SCCM who gives the go ahead for 'green-light boarding' to the dispatcher. That bit usually lasts between ten and twenty minutes.

Pre-boards/ wheelchair pax and any 'lift-ons' arrive first followed shortly after by all others; drinks served to premium cabin (s), baggage stowed in overhead lockers, captain's welcome onboard announcement, headcount, confirm all on, doors closed.

Pushback, doors to automatic and cross-checked, air con stops, engine no.1 start, lights flicker, safety demo followed by cabin secure passed onto the flight crew by inter-phone/ card slid across the door, (in person through the flight deck door in the good old pre 9/11 days), rumble along the taxi way for an age and await the double chimes of the seatbelt signs for imminent take-off by which time you should be strapped in unless you've totally misjudged it – hey, don't worry we've all done it! – and we're off, the engines whining on the take-off run, before the gentle V1 point of no-return and rotation, being airborne followed by the clunking sound of the landing gear being retracted into the solid belly of the airliner.

The senior's "Ladies and gentlemen, please remain seated..." PA is followed by a flurry of activity: the familiar busy galley noises of bar boxes being opened and slammed shut, drinks trolleys being un-padlocked and bev-makers being switched on. Meanwhile the plane banks to one side climbing to its initial allotted flight level, a sudden air pocket catching you unawares as you continue to soar above the clouds and into sunshine. The swish of curtains separating the classes always feels like a 'them and us' moment, the segregation causing those behind to wonder what exactly is so special on the other side....

Then the hard work starts. Every now and then there might be a spillage, and only the pax with the keenest eyes will ever notice a hand appear from the galley, at the base of the curtain, fumbling about for that elusive lost meal – the one that fell out of the oven. Once they're fed and watered, there's usually a duty free style service or another drinks round depending on the length of the flight, and possibly even more food. You do all that, then you encounter 'top of descent', clear-in, cabin secure, close curtains, 'congratulate' yourselves in the galley (ah, the good old days before everything became so serious) and take your jump seats for landing. Let's imagine then that you've been trained and are finally 'online'. What can you expect and why do people actually want to do this job? Here's what I've worked out, misconceptions included....

Misconceptions

"It looks glamorous and fun." It is not glamorous, but the appearance of a whole troupe of flight and cabin crew uniformed-up, with neck-scarves, swept-up hair, metal wings, gold stripes and long legs parading through an airport, can lead one to think that actually it *must* be glamorous, to get on a large aircraft that could be taking you anywhere across the globe, ending up next to a swimming-pool, sipping a cocktail and wearing Gucci sun-glasses, looking effortlessly beautiful. That's the imagination coupled to a little bit of truth only. Yes, I have sat beside many swimming pools in my time, trying to look beautiful in my cheap shades, but I think my favourite pool is in my own hometown where I play hide-and-seek with my kids. (The thrill of the chase, oh yes!) And I do have quite long legs. Flying is, however, tiring. Exhausting is a more fitting description and fatigue is common, but you just deal with it until you can do it no longer. Baldy B told me a medical 'fact' that she had chanced upon: A 40 year old air hostess had died and the autopsy revealed her organs resembled those of a woman twice her age. Easy to believe, as flying can be damaging to your health. Cabin air- conditioning systems are packed with bacteria, and the recycled air has been the cause of drowsiness among working cabin crew, while pax don't tend to notice as they are sitting down. You have a 50% higher risk of contracting one of several types of cancer and, at the very least, long-haul C/As have their circadian rhythms messed about with weekly.

Is it fun? Depends on who you work with on the day, and that could be completely unpredictable. You might end up with an introverted misery-guts who drains the life from you, and you have to work with them for maybe 10 or 12 hours. That however, is unlikely, as cabin-crew are chosen for their buoyancy and their energy – they'll be as happy at the end of a duty as they were when they started. The work is pretty straightforward: giving out food, drink and information – oh, and being personally responsible for about fifty peoples' overall safety. It doesn't stop there: you have to be a compliance officer, a nurse, a listener, a confidante, perceptive, alert, in-control and an ambassador for the company. Smiling helps a lot.

"You're just a waitress in the sky!" Groan… yes, maybe I am just a waitress in my black skirt, with an order pad in my white apron, who happens to be in the sky. (Been there, done that, but I think you'll find the male version is 'waiter.') I don't, however, recall the agony of learning about cultural requirements, multiple aircraft systems, hijack and safety procedures for exams in any waiter-training I did, if I had any waiter-training at all. Granted, I might convey food from one place to another, and I do operate at a height of around 35,000ft at a typical cruising speed of about 580 miles per hour, but I think it would be fair to say that a waiter/waitress would not have to go through the same rigorous national selection process and intensity of training as I and all of my international colleagues had to do. "Sick-bag, Madame?"

"Tea, coffee or me?" Other people write so candidly about their exploits, that I may conserve whatever dignity I may have, and ignore this one... Girls, over to you.

"You meet famous people." Yes, from time to time, and they normally just want to get on and work or sleep. Some 'famous people' are not household names: they could be writers, dignitaries, eminent researchers, play-wrights or even ex-offenders. We often mistake fame as being the sole preserve of anyone from Kanye through to Cheryl (surname to-be-decided). Best to leave your pax to it and to try to respectfully treat them the same as everyone else.

"Travel perks." Yes, it's true that every dog has its day ("... and a big dog-two days!" as octogenarian Arthur once told me...). The long-recognised travel industry perk of cut-price travel involves a certain amount of calculated risk. When I worked in the industry there were two main ticket types: the 'ID80' staff ticket representing an 80% discount off standard fare and in effect, as firm a voucher as you could get, apart from the fact that if the airline had to, they could bump you off in favour of full-fare paying pax. The 'ID90' was a true S/BY (standby) ticket which, on the one side, might allow you to get to the States and back for

£120 all in and the high chances of an upgrade to Business Class or even First but, on the other side, leave you with the anxiety of not getting onto the return flight at all. Perfect for single people with limited responsibilities. That was the stressful 'high' which you might experience when at the departure gate, waiting for your name to be called. I always managed somehow to get onto my flights, even those where the S/BY queue seemed to be longer than the pax queue. Prayer always worked. I could fly to Athens (ATH) C-class for about £56 return. Toronto (YYZ) cost us about £95 return: outbound (O/B) Canadian Airlines, inbound (I/B) BA Club World. (New York JFK by Concorde one-way saved me over £5,000, as that journey sector cost me only £410.)

As an example, three of us decided one day that as we had the same days off, Rich, Demetrius and I should 'conquer Europe' – in other words, pop up to the staff travel office, blind-pick a destination for the fun of it and leave that day. Romaine in Staff Travel was as frosty as ever and, having checked the loads and issued the tickets, haughtily looked me up and down through her horn-rims: "The '632' leaves LHR for FCO (Fiumcino, Rome) at midday – overbooked by three in Club – you won't get on looking like *that*..." Well, two and a half hours later, it was a case of me and my two friends sat in Club Europe on a 767, with a friendly hostess asking me, "More champagne, Mr Marton?" I could only respond cheerfully: "Yes, please!" I imagined how sourly Romaine might have looked if she could see me then.

"Working on the 'planes." Even standing next to a Boeing 737, the 'baby' of the Boeing generations, makes you realise that you are quite small yourself. When you consider that even such an airliner containing maybe 130 to 180 seats, starts at around £70m, you understand that it is slightly more than just a metal tube with seats in it, even though I use that expression myself from time to time... The draw for many people is that working around aircraft is a specialism, and the functions of an aeroplane are inherently interesting. So if you can get your foot in the door of this industry, you will be privy to insider facts, experiences, mishaps and openings that you wouldn't necessarily get anywhere else. Plus you'll never know "if this is going to be the day that...". It keeps you on your toes. You can also be secure in the knowledge that if anything serious happens at 'normal' work, it will probably be confined to the workplace and can be managed in-house. If anything serious happens with an airliner, it usually makes international news – and my aircraft disaster scrapbook. Have I come close to anything serious? Yes, I have had some near-misses, but with about 2,000 flight sectors under my belt, nothing major, although the *Daily Mail* and *The Sun* would have been most interested.... I'll tell you about those moments as we build up speed.

"Passengers" – aka pax. Yes, the good old fare-paying customers, who pay our wages and so on.... If you don't like helping people, then this industry is definitely the wrong one for you. In just a few weeks of flying, it is possible to interact with more people than most interact with in a lifetime, which gets you used to most personality types, requests, demands and problems to be solved. I'll explain this more in Chapter Six – Passenger Psychology – but I rarely had any problems I couldn't sort out or pass on successfully. I think that's probably because you can't afford to take the role too seriously; it's only flying after all and ludicrous that we are actually this high up – and still breathing. Get this into perspective and Mr Jones in 'two-delta' can easily be won over. You won't always get it right, but you will live to fight another day.

Salaries, slides and speed

I was always interested in the actual mechanics of the industry and how a plane works, more than how long a bev-maker takes to brew a pot of tea, but the following facts might well engage you…. You can join the airlines as a flight attendant (F/A) from aged eighteen. The average salary of a UK-based junior F/A is about £18,000 per annum, including flight allowances, and increases noticeably with seniority. I found out that many junior crew on old contracts at BA's main base LHR, could be drawing two to three times that amount. Seniors (SCCMs) on old contracts could earn a base salary of usually £40-64,000, dependent on fleet, at the same airline's main base. Typical salaries for the middle-eastern carriers like Emirates, Qatar and Etihad are around £20,000. Judging by some of the horror stories I have read, there are plainly many who regret joining these set-ups owing to the restrictive and oppressive regimes that are apparently in-force. Electronic monitoring, harsh rules and even curfews. All that glitters is not gold, and there's a lot of gold in the Middle East....

Should you forget to properly disarm the slide by falling into distracting conversation just when you should be cross-checking that your doors are in manual, then the cost of blowing the escape slide is heavy. Depending on A/C type, it's anywhere between £5,000 and £20,000 for a blown slide to be repacked by engineers. This is always at the back of your mind pre-pushback and post-departure, so door-checks are a sobering moment, hence the pins and flags on the doors as visual reminders. There is a now infamous story of an American male C/A on a JetBlue departure in 2010, having had enough of arguing with a customer, and vacating the jet by blowing a slide, but not before he had absconded with beers from the bar trolley. Good show, that man, but shame you got caught: it was somewhat inevitable, but one to tell the grandchildren – if you ever have them.

Again, something I shouldn't really be disclosing but not that long ago, I was distracted whilst we were taxiing, and overlooked a couple of things whilst my colleague Rob carried on with the demo in the forward cabin of the A320. The inter-phone went and I looked up instinctively to see a red light indicating the captain: "Simon, could you do us a favour and check Door 1R? It's not showing up as armed – it's probably the handle, just wiggle it, sometimes they get stuck, thanks." Er, the handle was not stuck, it was still in manual – the joys of cross-checking your doors, by yourself as two heads are better than one. I narrowly missed doing the demo myself as Rob was giving me discreet yet wild prompts with Jim Carrey-style facial expressions. I also didn't bother giving a "seats for take-off" call to the crew. It happened to be the day a safety inspector was auditing our flight, and would have been aware of everything. Even more sobering was the fact that I was the SCCM. We all get things wrong, and no harm done. I still had a job. We carried on to take off as normal.

An Airbus A320's typical take off speed is 150 knots (170 mph), whilst its landing speed averages 130-140 knots (about 150mph). Contrast this with a jumbo jet (B747) and a fully loaded one rotates into the air at about 160 knots (or 180mph), landing with significantly less fuel weight at its destination, with a speed of between 150-70 knots (or 170-195mph). Concorde used to take off at a much higher speed; I tell people that it took off like a rocket, which essentially it was – a stunning 220 knots (250 mph), landing at around 160 knots (185mph). Equivalent to Formula One in the 'airliner world'. Speaking of which, there is actually is such a magazine – some people don't believe me, but it is on sale at major high street outlets, such as WHSmith. I bought many issues, mainly for the centrefolds – *"Cor! A 737-200!"*

Magazines aside, and back into the real world. Next, I'll take you further into how the reluctant air-steward's journey unfolded....

Chapter Three

A 'proper' airline

When you get your foot in the door of an industry, seize a little experience and gain some confidence, it becomes much easier to move on to something seemingly better. The truth is that sometimes what looks good on paper can end up promising more than it delivers, like the C (business-class) main course served in a china bowl that actually tastes no better than an ECY (economy) foil-wrapped meal. Does the Champagne taste better in a glass flute, than a plastic tumbler? I wouldn't know – I swig directly from the bottle. When you work in the world of charter, you quickly realise that the scheduled airlines are the ones who offer the classier in-flight service: free drinks, lemon wedges pre-cut by caterers, china coffee cups with biscuits and a choice of newspapers from *The New York Times* to the *Financial Times* and all points in between. Charter operators are always playing catch-up owing to the different sector (no pun intended) that they are catering for. A holiday flight is a different beast from a scheduled flight, even though the cans are still miniature and they cruise at the same flight-levels. It's like comparing a Ford Focus to a Mercedes C-class. (Ahem, pun intended.)

I couldn't have been happier, nor my parents more proud of me than when I secured another contract at LGW, this time with the airline I had originally applied to work with at Bristol Airport: *Air 2000*. Looking back, that was a questionable name for an airline, not least as someone asked, "What happens when we reach the millennium? Do you have to change the name?!" They had apparently already thought of it and were lining up a brand name streamlining the holiday company branding too. Now, having passed the interview and signed the paperwork, I was working for a 'proper airline' – at least if you judge by the detailed organisation, for example, I was to attend an appointment at the city's *Moss Bros.* where I would be fitted for my new uniform. Dark suit, almost black with light striping, white shirt with thin red stripes and a red striped tie. It looked way better than I describe... honest.

Come the time for the *Ab Initio* training course of almost six weeks at a centre near the industrial estates in Crawley, Gatwick, I was waiting to be truly impressed. There were about 24 of us I remember, from various pathways;- a hairdresser to an administrative assistant, a few airport ground agents to a handful of previous flyers and even a model from New Zealand. The cabin-service training was a most needlessly lengthy and complicated process, which detailed how "you use that single cart from its stowage at the rear galley to meet the R3 crew member to swap with the L2 cart at D1R in order to continue the service from row 11 backwards", etc.... The former salon owner broke down in tears and I wasn't surprised. The main trainer, caked in make-up, resembled an example of artificial intelligence, devoid of any empathy, because her obvious single purpose was to achieve completion of the course by dutifully speeding all of the candidates through to 'wings day' and thereby return to BHX (Birmingham) and flying duties as a SCCM – and her boyfriend. The only part of the course I really enjoyed was the safety element which was about two weeks long and included the 757 aircraft visit, swimming pool drills, the mock-up, slide-jumps and equipment training at Monarch HQ, Luton Airport. Oh, and I met my future girlfriend there, but in retrospect, it was a road I should not have travelled, as we were made for entirely different paths…. (I really wanted to be a session drummer, whilst she wanted to save donkeys. See?)

And so arrived 'wings day' in late November, and we, as two classes, passed out as Grade 4 juniors, clothed in red and black, with new updated and extended one-year fixed-term contracts. That meant confirmed employment, but no extras like holidays. Once 'online' (working), I could expect the usual mix of Mediterranean there-and-backs, ski-flights to Geneva and the odd mainland Europe. Our rosters came through and the unthinkable happened which made myself and Kim, a fellow new entrant, the envy of many. Incredibly, for my first flying duties I had been allocated a five day trip, to include Paris then onto Berlin and home featuring night stops in Paris, Newcastle, Leeds and a day-stop in the German capital. This type of duty was unheard-of and caused a ripple of discontent amongst the regular long-term crew community.

Paris, Berlin and a ballet-dancer demo

When I checked in for my briefing, the senior who was unusually
pleasant, handed us all £80 cash to cover expenses for the first two
days, in the same way as a band on tour, before we had even sat
down. I had a feeling this was going to be a good few days and I
wasn't wrong. Post-briefing and dressed in smart casuals for a
positioning flight, the nine of us checked in for a Brit Air flight in a
Canadair Learjet-type plane to Nantes, Northern France.
Something about the intimacy of the small commuter jet and the
lone French air steward with ginger hair struck a chord with me
(probably a G), and I ear-marked this experience. He kissed the
ground agent girl on both cheeks as he closed up, and I recall his
brilliant pirouette behind everyone's backs at the rear of the
aircraft as he danced his way through the safety demo. The flight
was short and sweet – only about 45 minutes or so, and Rudolf
Nureyev gave me an extra whisky miniature too, so I took a selfie
with him on exit to record the event. The purpose of the trip was
that we had been subbed out to cover Air Inter (Air France's
partner airline) internal flights owing to a strike by their crews over
pay. The work was going to be minimal, starting at 06:00 and
finishing around 10:00 over the two days, leaving us free for good
food, a couple of bars and a trip to the Eiffel Tower where the
F/O Paul caught me off guard. I was in pensive mood near a
railing 300 metres up overlooking the capital, and he suddenly
grabbed me by the shoulders which caused my heart to stop

momentarily as I muttered a couple of moderate expletives. (A similar thing happened to me when my friend Rich pushed me onto the glass flooring section of the CN Tower, Toronto, causing me to scream in front of about ten Japanese girls. They laughed as they filmed me and thus Anglo-Japanese relations were maintained as stable.)

The nine of us, save myself, Kim and the captain John, parted company after Paris as we returned to LGW in an empty 757 loaded with pastries and free beers from the Air Inter bars, and smiles on our faces at how we had trumped the system. From there, the three of us flew up to Newcastle within the hour and night-stopped there, ready for a very early flight the following morning with a Manchester crew of six personnel joining us. We flew across to Leeds Bradford to pick up a full load of two hundred and thirty three day-trippers wanting to go to Berlin. The upshot was that we also went to Berlin for a full day too, and, being December it was Christmas market time, with the late afternoon atmosphere being slightly magical, with the glow of holy candles and the smell of marzipan in the air.

I checked in at the five star hotel which was either a Crowne Plaza or an Intercontinental. Once inside the room, having popped my bags away, I picked up the remote and switched on the box which displayed the message "Welcome Mr Simon Marton to Berlin; we hope you enjoy a pleasant stay with us." "What a friendly TV!" I thought to myself before retiring to the bathroom to start clearing out the free shampoo, conditioner and soap bottles.

Berlin was grey and cold, but it felt reassuring to be part of a small group of experienced 'tourists', now in civvies using the yellow *U-Bahn* underground, taking in the sights of a city I had heard so much about for all the wrong reasons. The day passed quickly and we departed about 21.00 after being de-iced at the freezing airport, climbing steeply into dark blizzard skies. On climb out, now probably around 1,500ft, the engine volume suddenly dropped, as I and the girl sitting next to me at R2 exchanged a slightly worried look. I realised that this was noise abatement, a totally normal procedure that spared residents below a little pain from constant jet noise overhead. At least this wasn't the 1970's when turbojet engine technology produced 150db (decibels) as standard with streams of black smoke behind. In comparison, the 757 was a fairly clean model with state of the art systems and apparently an improved carbon footprint. Everyone knows now that it's still a 'dirty jet' that may be slightly cleaner than others, but it's still no angel. Leeds passed without incident and it was a coach trip for just the three of us back to LGW the following day. Regarding duties, it was back to normal at Air 2000 – regular Gran Canaria, Tenerife, Malaga and ski flights. Regimented, slick, professional and dull. The only thing I would look forward to were notes left in my pigeon-hole by my then girlfriend who worked for the same company as we passed each other by like ships in the night – literally.

Back on the ground, I was renting rooms in the area, and had moved twice in seven months. Baldy B kept in contact, and I went to see her one frosty evening for a catch-up and a glass of red. Whatever house I ended up in, if there was multiple-crew occupancy there was always a bottle open. Between flights in these houses, girls were often seen in white towelling robes, covered in face cream and sporting cucumber slices over their eyes. Then they would undo all the work by caning it through a couple of bottles of *Blossom Hill*. She was between trips to IAD (Washington DC) and NRT (Narita, Japan), and was staying over at one of the two terraced cottages usually rented out for crew in Horley, a half a mile from the airport. As we talked, the sound of creaking floorboards suggested someone walking across one of the bedrooms upstairs. She stopped talking and asked slowly, "Did you hear that just then?" I nodded. "Simon, there's absolutely no-one else here in either of the cottages; they're all away on trips!" It was a '*Twilight Zone*' moment, and as we breathed deeply, we poured a little more Shiraz and resigned ourselves to the fact that the owner of the footsteps had achieved the desired effect.

There were a couple of rooms going in a beautiful quaint barn conversion opposite the cottages, and I am not quite sure was ever a barn in the first place, but little matter. Four of us (Baldy, Rich, Blodders and me) occupied the single storey 'barn' and enjoyed a happy enough time there for the best part of a further nine months. Three air-hostesses and a firefighter – a mix which worked as we all understood each other's worlds and rosters. We never did find out if the barn was haunted too.

My wings are clipped

"Up, up and away" went the song, except I was not in a balloon: I was in a modern Boeing 757, part of an 18-strong fleet which exuded quality, reputable branding and strong organisation. In truth, I hated it and I was not alone. There was a strong underlying feeling of needless discipline, a stiffness to every flight which made it feel like a military exercise and a hierarchical structure for the cabin crew to observe. Looking back, I know why: I had come from an outfit that was shoddy by comparison, but where we had had to rally together to pull through every day, to ensure that the bad moods and low impressions of the passengers on entering the cabin were transformed into smiles and gratitude on exit, and there was something really special about that. The contrast here was that the standards were so high, there was no room for error, almost as if they didn't know what a bad day could possibly look like.

The cabin service was – and still is – the pride of the charter airlines world, with awards fought over yearly to see who could provide the best experience and the most innovative in-flight product. In reality, my feeling remains the same: it's the quality of the flight attendants and the way in which we interact with customers, that determines how successful a flight has been, along with the actual pilot-handling-quality. You could throw a multitude of gimmicky plastic emblazoned items, or provide a hot-chocolate service on ski-flights (wow!), but it's the personal touch in the delivery that provides the difference, hence you can tell my disregard for awards, as they will come and go anyway. On the odd days I was allowed to be myself, I found that my comic outlook, such as japing with the Greek smokers on video at the back on a night-flight from Athens, and even using my rude Greek vocabulary, helped lift an average atmosphere into a great one, causing people to write 10/10 satisfaction cards.

I recall a routine day-flight to TFS where I was working around the middle of the 757 and a group of elderly couples from London started bantering with me. It started with me handing out hot towels from a tray, and remarking, "These look like something from my mum's undies drawers..." Once they had finished chuckling, one guy said, "It looks like an 'Always Ultra', Simon!" (You see, I knew a little about feminine hygiene.) My reply: "Yes, look Mum- Simon, with wings!" (I believe you might still find the advert online and you'll appreciate my double-entendre.) The other chap giggled as he asked me: "Eh, Simon – have you joined the mile-high club?!" Knowing that this was going to be risqué, I decided to curtail my conversation with a 'no-comment' reply, which always seemed to work when the suspect was questioned on *The Bill*, or, more recently *Line of Duty*. I saw how my particular section was a merry little cabin and that sector ended up with a job offer from a couple on leaving the aircraft, who had been watching my interactions throughout the whole four-hour flight. However, for many flights I felt my own wings had been needlessly clipped, and I was itching to leave after only five months. I also kept hitting my head on the retractable TV aft of the forward galley.

That was probably the main reason for handing in my notice. That, and the following which put the final nail in the coffin for me. I wrote a note before an early check-in to one of my former pilot colleagues, Ray, who owned a Honda Goldwing 1500. Having parked my own motorbike under the bike shelter at the roadside end of the runway threshold of 2-6 Left, I tucked the note into his windshield. It read: *"Dear Ray, saw your bike and hope you're doing well...I'm at Air 2000 -but not really enjoying it, and I'm looking elsewhere as I write. Can't wait to leave. Hope all's well with you, cheers, Simon (ex-Goldcrest.)"* Turns out that of all the bikes I could have chosen to leave the note upon, I had picked the wrong one. That Goldwing happened to belong to the Base Manager of... yes, Air 2000. Ray and Martin owned similar bikes. How was I to know? It was dark at 05:45. I would like to think that this airline might question the moderate leaving rate of new entrants, but as with other organisations, there was no time for that, as a steady supply of fresh candidates were itching to join.

Someone had tipped me off that Cityflyer Express, a BA franchisee, were after experienced cabin crew and the biggest draw for me was… small aircraft. That flight to Nantes with Brit Air had made a big impression on me, for there was a guy who made it his own, played by his own rules and was free to be himself with no-one looking over his shoulder or breathing down his neck. The pirouette could be worked on, the miniatures were free and the Canadair they operated resembled a private jet. Who wouldn't want a job like that? The reluctant air-steward knew it was time to ditch the charter-airline scene of night-flights and hideously early check-ins and delays, in order to experience the more upmarket and perhaps slicker flying experience that the scheduled airlines offered. In other words, no check-ins in the middle of the night, a darker uniform, permanent contracts with travel perks, and maybe pax who were less brusque….I soon returned my uniform, flight bag and black leather gloves, but kept my metal wings as I had earned those.

City-flying

Welcome to the more intimate world of city-flying. I had applied and ended up in another hotel room, being interviewed for the third time in less than a year. I was frank, yet polite and was duly offered a full-time permanent contract, subject to the usual six month probation period. I sported the BA uniform which included a tie clip(!), an embroidered woven wing, and a much-loathed 'in-flight jacket' for male 'stewardesses', which was rarely worn, as it was simply too hot and too cumbersome in tiny cabins. It turned out it was usually discarded across all the BA fleets from 737's to

Jumbos, unless the senior was 'by the book'. The original LGW Airport building was known as The Beehive, because… you can probably guess why. It existed in the Twenties and Thirties, and was still being used for training staff and as a meetings venue when I joined my third airline, which turned out to have the second highest aircraft movements at the airport, after BA itself. *Cityflyer Express* was a small friendly company with the feel of an extended family. The crew-offices (four pre-fabricated buildings joined together) were near the bottom of the Iain Stewart Centre where GB (Gibraltar) Airways were also based. The pre-fabs were accessed by wooden decking style steps where a trio of LDV minibuses were based, driven by several ex-firemen, each with their own set of stories to tell and dirty jokes which sometimes rivalled aircrews' own. They were only just out-smoked by cabin-crew and pilots.

I can only recall mainly happy times working there for an outfit that had 'propellor planes' while nearly everyone else had jets. ATR stood for *Avion de Transport Regionale*, but you had to learn to call them 'advanced turboprops'. BA Euro-Gatwick which operated 737s laughed at the ATRs, which is probably what BA main-line who operated jumbo-jets, in turn did to 737s. It's called 'the mine's bigger than yours syndrome.' It always felt ridiculous calling a stubby old ATR42 an 'airliner', but that's what it was – it just didn't have the kudos of a 747 or even a Fifties' Comet. (Dan Air still had one floating about then, on the remote stands near the control tower.) We were a franchise of BA so were to the fare-paying punter, corporately the same airline. It was during training that we discovered how belonging to a brand meant that ticket prices could be set to astronomical levels by the mother-ship, just because they could. For example, we were horrified to learn that a 40-minute flight to Jersey could extract over £400 return from someone's wallet, instead of the £150 we considered fair for such a relatively short journey. This was in the days before the low-cost acts dominated the scene, so carriers like BA held the monopoly, and pax either flew or found some other way of getting to their destinations, such as coach, ferry, train or bicycle.

The training mercifully lasted two weeks less than Air 2000's drawn-out five-week affair and, pretty soon, I was online once more hitting the skies of Ireland, Germany, Switzerland, Holland, Belgium, the Channel Islands and even Leeds Bradford again, cruising at a level of 22,000 feet. In those days, the turboprop's advantage over a jet was the lower operating ceilings meaning shorter and more efficient climbs/descents, on paper anyway. The ATR was a funny little thing: the pilots were trained to land it in a particular fashion – steep approach, pull up at the last second and then push forward the yoke with three clunks to make sure it was firmly down on the runway and couldn't be a victim of the wind trying to bounce it back in the air. Having said that I couldn't understand why the visiting *Islandsflug* (Icelandic airline) to whom we had subbed out some work, managed to land their ATR's as smoothly as silk compared to our lot. Doubtless the vodka helped.

The Scandinavian countrymen could always handle their drink better than most.

At the point I joined the airline, there was some excitement as orders had just been placed for a couple of Avro RJ100 'Whisper jets' with another two further down the line, due to route expansion and passenger demand. These were 'proper' commuter jets, also called 'pocket rockets', that were modelled on the Bae '146' airliner that had been a global success story for British Aerospace. Avro, based in Woodford near Manchester, had also made, among other planes, the WW2 Lancaster bomber, so were of strong heritage. The RJ stopped short of dropping bombs, though. It was perfect for short runways with a STOL ability (short take-offs and landings) as demonstrated on Saturday-morning chartered ski-flights to Chambery Savoie Mont Blanc (CMF). The tarmac runway measured just over 2,000m long, so the RJ would taxi to the threshold and wait for clearance for departure. The next bit was quite impressive even for us C/As. Full power was applied with brakes set, until released: we would literally be shaking in our seats feeling the four helicopter engines roaring to make use of the limited runway, with only one chance to get it right and soar clear of the mountain range.

We were landing into ZRH (Zurich) one winter's morning when I sensed that perhaps the landing was just a little too smooth and too perfect. I shared with the pax my sneaking feeling that the plane had landed itself, and seconds after I had finished my PA, sure enough Capt. Johnson confirmed to all onboard that I was right and the plane had used the *Auto-land* feature which they tested every now and then. (*Auto-land* was first used on British Tridents in the 1970s I believe.) The French-built ATR 42 and 72 were still the mainstay of the fleet and we had 13 of them in the two years I was there. 'Cute', 'stubby', 'intimate', 'toy-town' and even 'hairdryers' were some of the adjectives applied to the ATR. Both the front and rear baggage holds could be accessed at cabin-level through cargonets, somewhat reminiscent of WW2 bombers. Personally, I liked them, especially for the complete change of feel from the far larger aircraft I had experience of working on. Talking of bombs, there was around that time a visiting Russian chartered aircraft, with an antique-looking front end, heavy on glass window panels top and bottom, that looked at odds with every other 'normal' airliner out on the ramp. It was always parked remotely from the main terminals and looked like a bulldog that had crashed the poodles' party. Jason UFG had already given me the lowdown on the strange-looking glass-fronted Ilyushin prop-liner: "They're ex-military planes and can be converted back into a bomber in about 20 minutes." That was reassuring to know.

Lodged in a special receptacle at the back of the ATR 72 next to the rear door with built-in stairs is a thick metal tube maybe a metre long, with a point at the bottom end. The deal is that once you have arrived at your destination, you hand it to the greeting ground agent once you have opened the door – (either electrically operated or manual) and you see them disappear beneath you. They emerge with a smile and a thumbs up for disembarkation to commence. The tail prop is in place to prevent the aircraft from tipping up onto its tail during boarding and disembarking, as the weight transfers to the rear. The French – they think of everything, not just the snails. I'm half-Italian, but call me a *'rosbif'* if you like.

The nature of city-flying was quite different from charter. The joy of scheduled flying for a national carrier brand is that you can almost be guaranteed you're back at home most nights. You also have night stops away from home, the main draw being that you check in for work late afternoon, so have that day to do your own thing, carry out your outbound sector no more than an hour or two, stay the night in a hotel and operate the first flight back in the morning, giving you the rest of the day off. A couple of hours catch-up sleep sorts you out on returning home, leaving you time to go to Tesco or simply wander around the shops.

Yet no airline is immune to delays, bomb scares or bad weather, and just because you have the heritage of the national flag distinctively painted on the tail-plane, it doesn't mean there won't be problems. The crews all pulled together on first-name terms and in the main were very friendly. There were characters of course – from the captain who liked to play the *Thunderbirds* theme through the PA at the take-off position, to the hostie who fancied herself as Zsa Zsa Gabor, elaborately over-pronouncing *"Darling"* to everyone, and regaling those within earshot of her party tricks. In truth, I think she may have been covering over the fact that she had a normal life of tea and digestives, and just wanted to impress. Some of the straight guys were taking their PPLs (private-pilots licences), as were a couple of girls. The other guys were mainly a mix of drama-queens, clubbers, party animals or simply quiet. Always watch the quiet ones.

This next bit, I shouldn't really be telling you, but in effect that's probably most of this book. Because we were so pressed for time on these short-hops, on a there-and-back, you would quickly realise that the bars containing alcohol and duty-free goods would have to be counted, padlocked and sealed before landing at LGW, the same as any other flight landing into the UK for Customs and Excise rules. It was quite common to be sitting at the back of the ATR with a bar trolley unsecured and open, counting the contents of each drawer individually, entering the closing stock on the C209 customs paperwork whilst announcing the "Ladies and gentlemen, British Airways Express welcomes you to London Gatwick, where the local time is…." PA. This of course defied any safety rules but it was the only way you could get the work done without facing the threat of arrest at LGW by HM Customs. Bar trolleys are heavy by nature – even the single carts – and one of these unsecured could easily break a limb at landing speed, the only saving grace being that the aircraft were too small to be equipped with escape slides. Still, we managed to do this as senior crew and it was an unmentioned yet acknowledged routine aspect of flying such short sectors. Along with other 'traditions' that will remain kept to ourselves, such as the legend of 'LDs'.

It was here at this airline that I discovered the delights of an APT S/BY (airport standby) on your roster. Operationally, it made sense that because planes can break ('go tech'), at least one fully crewed aircraft on standby was a necessity to provide the cover should another one fail to deliver the goods. APT S/BY's could typically last six to eight hours and the worst bit was being called out right at the last minute, or say within twenty minutes of finishing, which is why I tended not to plan anything in the evenings just in case. That's one of the unwritten things about the job: you feel somewhat beholden to your employer and it overtakes much of your normal life, but that's the nature of the employment. Aircraft fly all over the world and dot the skies from early mornings over Finland before the sun rises to the middle of starry nights across China. Crews the world over are looking after the safety, comfort and wellbeing of pax who are simply taking their journeys at whatever time of day. An AOG (Aircraft on the ground) is not making money for the company which is why it has to make several rotations per day on average – if we take a day as being a full 24 hours. They are designed to be used and used until they can no longer be profitably abused any longer. Then they are either scrapped or retired and often end up on the African continent, where they might enjoy fewer restrictions on engine noise and could maybe give another ten years' service to their owners. If you're wondering where all the smokey old 1-11s, 737s, 757s, DC10s and Tristars end up, look down on the map and try Nigeria, Ethiopia, Zaire and South Africa for starters. (Someone has even converted an old Olympic Airways 727 into his home deep in the woods of Oregon, USA.) Airliners are worked until they give up and cannot go on any longer. A little like me in my uniform and shiny black shoes. Just give me my orders, tell me where you want me to go, but as long as I get a warm mini-croissant from the basket, one of those bacon-and-egg rolls from the forward galley oven, and maybe an orange juice in a real glass with a real orange slice, then I am yours, O' airline...

Chapter Four

Terror in the skies (or when things go wrong...)

Just like the vintage Ford Capri 2.8 *Ghia* that Uncle Del lovingly restores every weekend, a 25-year-old aircraft is going to need more TLC and spares than a ten-year-old example, even though they are both work-horses. Every now and then (but it did seem to be more like 'every now'), G-CEAP, our beloved Tristar, which had a knack of going 'tech', would need an engineering check at exactly the time it was supposed to be on the taxiway heading for the CAT 3 hold (category 3 holding point) of Runway 26L, fully laden with eager punters wanting some Mediterranean sun. A typically used engineering phrase was: "Alpha Papa's offline owing to a three-hour ramp-check." What does this mean in English? "The plane needs a proper fix and it ain't going nowhere for a while. Have a seat, and put the coffee on."

Such a shame, because the L1011 in full airborne mode is a glorious sight, even with its engines whining as it ascends gracefully into the summer skies. I recall one morning – just prior to boarding the regular early am Malaga (AGP) which I always seemed to be rostered – the double trolleys bearing all 400 Daily Mails were pulled out of sight of pax for a hushed reason. On the front page was a photo of one of our rivals' Tristars, with a headline indicating safety issues and the business going under. The phrase used by the paper was "To be grounded." We happened to be parked right next to one of them and were operating the same aircraft (A/C) type. The withdrawal of the paper saved some questions, and ensured that we had a chance of getting airborne close to on time, which for us, was often within four hours of the scheduled time of departure (STD), and usually longer.... So, on that occasion a light awkwardness had been averted and we certainly weren't going to be grounded. However, I've been in several situations where we came perilously close....

Lightning strikes

One morning in June 1996, we took off in the mist from Shannon, Ireland, carrying a full load of 393 Irish Catholics on a pilgrimage to CIA (Ciampino, Rome). Flight time: two and a half hours, weather: uncertain, even at 39,000 ft, and mood onboard: pleasant. Our onboard ageing 'Husky' sales computers weren't loaded, so we had to use the pen and paper/mental calculation of punts-to-pounds conversion. I seemed to have the knack of guesstimating these with the appearance of authority, so several of the girls on the other aisle were asking what the change should be on various drinks and duty-free transactions.

Twenty five minutes to go, and well into Italian airspace, the mood had changed palpably as we hit turbulence on the descent, and the big old bus was being buffeted suddenly and thrown awkwardly, like a staggering drunk. We had entered storms from the Mediterranean, so the outside clouds were thick and grey, and there was the odd flash as we continued to lose height. As we were making sure everyone was strapped in, I walked along the forward starboard section of the cabin when, without warning, a dramatic streak of lightning shot through the entire 50m length of the cabin, at just above head height. My first reaction – thankfully in my head – was "Wow – cool!" But even at 25 years old, I could plainly see that men and women at least double my age and older, were shaking, emotional, and in need of pacifying. My SCCM Tina looked over to me and mouthed: "Simon, KEEP SMI-LING!" So we did, and together watched the mood gradually change, as I saw various people chatting to each other in soft Dublin accents as they looked upon me: "Look, he's smiling, it's all right!"

Eventually the flight engineer gave the earlier-than-usual advice: "Cabin crew, it'd be wise to take your seats for landing now" and, as the giant liner was put into the flare, the fields around Ciampino came into view through the fog. As soon as the nose-wheels hit the tarmac, and the thrust reversers roared, there was a burst of applause and some cheering too, breaking the tension of the previous half hour. Everyone, except the crew, left the plane down covered stairs, and onto buses below which were waiting in sheet rain. We weren't out of trouble yet. The moody captain yelled in Michael Caine fashion: "Shut the bloody doors!" A small river was coursing to the flight deck, threatening to blow all the electrics and render the plane useless. Down slid the electrically operated door at 1 Left, sealing shut. We mopped up the excess water with paper towels, leaving an ex-RAF captain slightly less irate.

After breakfast, we departed from Rome within the hour, empty save for us crew members, into rapidly clearing skies. 'Michael Caine,' who had obviously been watching me in the window reflection by his captain's seat, turned around and snatched from my hand the map on which I had skilfully been entertaining Tina with my finger-compass across the continents. Maybe he should have blown the bloody doors off.

Missing a wheel

It was a regular flight out from LGW on an ATR 72 turboprop, with about 40 pax onboard. Flying conditions were good and there was nothing notable in the cabin, apart from the coffee cups not having been loaded onto the meal trays so we had to amend the service slightly. A 55 minute sector to RTM (Rotterdam) with nothing to report. We landed smoothly enough for an ATR and the pax disembarked. A 30-minute turnaround, during which the F/O did his walk around outside checking the aircraft condition. He returned five minutes later as white as a sheet. "We're missing a nose-wheel!" Two minutes later, both he and Brendan, the captain returned from the flight deck to add more good news: "We're going nowhere – Gatwick ATC radioed to confirm they saw something fall from us as we climbed out! They're sending an engineer and spares out now, so the plane's gone tech." We didn't night-stop, instead we bussed to AMS (Amsterdam) and took a sister-company flight home to London from there. With one nose-wheel gone, the array of outcomes could have been catastrophic: skidding, landing-gear collapse, belly-scraping down the runway, fire and at the very worst collision leading to death. No wonder he was white.

Called to a hotel

Fast forward to 14 years later. Picture a substantially older man, now at a desk in CRC (Crew Report Centre, T5 Heathrow) looking at a screen, inputting the same eight pieces of data relating to colleague sickness and trying to make it stretch another few hours until close of Sunday. I was on a 'ground duty day', a euphemism for "report to Heathrow and become a pseudo-HR manager for the day". Dull as ditchwater, and twice as painful to endure. *"God, please take me away from here – I'm so bored…"*. He answered my prayers at 14:12 local time that afternoon, in the knowledge I needed a new dimension to my day. I was referred on by another manager – Mark – to take on 'an incident' at a nearby crew hotel needing a male manager. "It could be a fight, or a rape. It could even be a death, but it won't be that."

Off I went with duty manager Ian, a genial man who like me, had worked on the Tristar years before, so we shared common ground. As we met with the Dutch hotel manager – a polite and confidence-inspiring gentleman with army peace-keeping experience in Lebanon – he announced to us in his car: "Gentlemen, there's been a death." (So much for Mark's advice.) Apparently, a crew member who was a regular at the hotel had not been seen in a day or two and a chamber-maid had raised the alarm after a funny smell was emanating from his bedroom. Over the next three hours, we drank three pots of tea served in white hotel china in his office, were interviewed by police, advised on the need for absolute silence until the coroner's report came out, and devised a plan for the discreet removal of the deceased crew-member's body from the hotel.

The private ambulance-men arrived, and between the three of us, we blocked off two corridors in the hotel under the premise of 'removing hazardous waste from a room'. The ambulance men worked quickly and efficiently, straining and sweating under the black suits they were wearing in the summer warmth, until the black bag appeared on a low trolley from the room. We bundled ourselves into a cramped service lift, quietly and respectfully, with the zipped body bag at our feet on the trolley. Within two minutes the van-doors were closed, hands were shaken and we disbanded. As we arrived back at T5, Ian suggested an extra couple of days off owing to what I had just had to deal with, and I seized them with gratitude. I was back on a fairly quiet M4 within 30 minutes, driving home, as the sun faded, bringing Sunday to a close.

I returned to LHR on the Thursday to resume duties, this time a long-haul trip. Pre-briefing, I thought I would wander over to the obituaries-board to check if the deceased had been added. Sure enough the announcement was there: a nickname referring to his tan, and a rough laser-copy of his face; it was then that it hit me. That body had a face, a history, a life, and sadness covered me like a cloak. In among the hustle and bustle of all these hundreds of personnel, I had a secret. Ian and I had been there at the hotel, and we had kept it under wraps for the sake of the family. Unbelievably, we had kept it so watertight, it had not leaked onto social media before his NOK (next-of-kin) were informed. It was a surreal moment that none of my smiling crew in the briefing room would ever be aware of. No foul play – cause of death was suspected deep vein thrombosis (DVT). This is what you usually expect to happen to pax, not cabin crew.

Trouble over Rio

I had been called out of standby at bang-on 09:00: "Simon we've got a report time of 11.00 for you: Rio, a three-day trip." Racing up to LHR, running through the report centre and signing-in on the computer, I made auto-check-in on the crew briefing terminal with just 30 seconds to go. Unusually, a couple of managers were there waiting for me, just in case they had to appoint a replacement SCCM to operate the flight, but the relief from my No. 4 (next in command) was obvious as it was only to be his second flight for the airline, and his nerves were racing anyway. The fact that he had infinitely more flying hours than me and just as much ability to lead a team was hard for him to understand: *"But this is BA!"* I told him to relax: "It's just another tail colour." He wasn't in the mood to relax, but a poolside table at Rio might help....

Once securely into the cruise, it was brought to my attention that someone had been smoking in the loo nearest the flight deck, but it couldn't be ascertained who exactly. The toilet is probably the worst place in the cabin to start a fire, as it can spread quickly and infiltrate panels, destroying vital cables along its course, so we carried fire axes and a jemmy (crow bar) as standard. I stepped into the flight deck for my usual bout of CRM (crew resource management) – to chat and bond with the pilots. The captain and I started a discussion on fire-fighting based on the smoking in the toilet we had been talking about, whilst the 777 smoothly flew the director on its course to South America. "Basically Simon, if you and your crew can't get a fire out within 20 minutes, we have to decide whether we let the plane break up in the air, or we slam it down into the ocean." He reached for a map, unfolding it, and using a pen to point to our current approximate location – 500 miles off the coast of Senegal, West Africa, heading over the South Atlantic. He continued: "And out here, they'd never find us." I suddenly felt incredibly vulnerable, small and insignificant. While people a few feet behind the flight deck door were reclining on flat beds, drinking Champagne or sleeping, I was being reminded that this giant of the skies was not even a pin-prick on a map. That's enough to silence any over-inflated ego – even in Business class.

The return sector the next evening proved to be little more demanding. On arrival at the aircraft, the captain and I met – this was a new crew rotation as the cabin crews were only given a night stop, unlike the flight crews' two-night stopovers. There had been a problem with the toilet-smoke detectors on the plane, therefore instead of a half-hourly 'all-is well' check, we agreed I would patrol and pass a 15 minute toilet-check, just to be on the safe side. It didn't impact the in-flight service as much as I thought and, within three hours, I had sent the first half of my crew up for their two-hour break.

Half the battle with these transatlantic night flights was staying alert. Eating fresh fruit packed for the crew often helped at about 03:00, as did unused Club-class desserts, but there's only so much cheesecake a man can handle in the middle of the night, even if it does have fresh kiwis and strawberries on top, drizzled with a fruit compote.

As it happened, it wasn't long before I was needed. My stand-in senior at the back of the aircraft called me down to have a look at the control panel screen which was displaying random pop-ups in typical crazed-computer fashion, while in the darkness of the cabin, the 'Exit' lights were flashing at several door stations. I returned to the flight deck to chat via radio to the engineers at Heathrow to get the authority to pull some circuit breakers for example. No go, as new procedures put paid to that idea. Back in the cabin, recalling that this was now about 4am, three of my first-break crew suddenly appeared well before their break was due to end, looking distressed. My No.4 frantically told me how an evacuation alarm had sounded upstairs in the bunks, and of how they had raced to get their clothes on, fearing a full-on emergency. I told them to relax as we had it covered – it was just a cabin-system fault. (The irony was not lost on me that it was the same journey ex-Rio, that an Air France A330 had made in 2009 before plummeting into the sea with the terrible loss of all life on board; a misreading of in-flight systems in the flight-deck.) The pax slept through the entire thing, blissfully unaware of anything and shortly afterwards, I followed suit. The cheesecake had eventually worn me down.

An emergency averted

"Med-link Phoenix, Speedbird 217; message totally unreadable."

That was the sixth time the captain had tried to contact our medical advice- partner based in Arizona, using VHF and UHF to no avail. The captain was training a first officer – she had previously been on the Airbus fleet, and was on a series of check-flights, converting to the 777. We all had our headsets on, trying to make out the garbled messages that the medical professional was giving us, writing down the drug name on pieces of paper so as to compare our results. A seven-year-old boy had been taken ill en route to Denver, violently sick with diarrhoea and showing no signs of improvement, so it looked as though we were facing the prospect of calling for a doctor to administer the drug from the controlled-use medical M2 case onboard. The alternative was to divert and, being over Greenland – a huge expanse of icy territory a few hours from Canadian airspace – this was our most likely destination.

The seven-year-old boy was travelling with his dad and older brother, the father deeply appreciative of all we were doing, but I wanted a simple result which didn't merit the drama and upheaval of a diversion to a remote airfield in the middle of nowhere. I quickly searched the manifest and found two doctors onboard. One was an Indian gentleman sat in Club World, who couldn't assist as he was a doctor of psychology, but sitting at the rear of the plane was a retired GP in her late 60s, travelling with her husband. She immediately identified the problem with her experienced eyes. Smiling, she said, "No need for injections, just give him some lemonade – it's 'D and V'. (Diarrhoea and vomiting). Check on him every 15 minutes." What a lovely lady. We monitored the boy who greatly improved, much to his father's relief especially. I asked the GP and her husband to follow me with their bags, and they continued the flight in relative luxury, enjoying a complimentary afternoon tea an hour before landing – the least I could do for them.

Ice-skating Fiesta

I thought I was being clever by copying Jason the engineer when the heavy snows came and shut down the airport in December '99. The whole of the apron at BRS had turned into an ice-rink, and I recall only three differently branded airliners parked on the ramp, unable to get to the party. Jason had used his Volvo and I was now using the company Fiesta. I had successfully pulled several handbrake skids in succession, as near to those aircraft as I dared to drive, each with a turning circle of about 25m, and the best one revolved the car three times before re-aligning. I was less Lewis Hamilton and more Lewis Collins in those moments, but was living the daydream. I had a radio and a car with a flashing light on top – what more could a man want? I returned joyfully to the ticket desk to tell the girls how much fun was to be had. Their reply? "We know. Security were watching you on their cameras." Oops.

Don't cross live runways

Typically, it's when you take the Phillips screwdriver out of your bag, and don't put it back, it's gonna be the next day you need it. Similarly, when Susie and I swapped dispatcher shifts, so she could do my Filton (FZO) airfield familiarisation day, and I could have her day off, how was I to know that it would be *me* who would have needed the training, and not her? The fog came down and BRS was closed to traffic, so I was ordered to drive across town to meet and greet our airliners, armed with the flashing-light vehicle and a company mobile phone. The plan was that I could relay basic info to the crews, so that we could arrange arrivals and departures from FZO, and limit disruption as far as possible.

I was having a great time. Flight-crews were happy to see a friendly face, I got used to the Nokia phone calls and the plan seemed to work. I was aware that the yellow Airfield Safety Unit (ASU) Land Rover was following me wherever I went, as I tried to follow procedures I knew from BRS as much as possible. I was going way faster than the 15mph speed limit, plus I ended up getting in the way of a couple of 'general aviation' planes on live taxiways, and had a polite telling off from the ASU.

However, the best bit came when I was over-concentrating on the car stereo, and as I looked up I screeched to a halt. I had only managed to stray onto the runway threshold with the low wall to my left. The flashing lights should have warned me, but I could hear the troubling sound of nearby jet engines idling. Looking to my right I did a double-take: two Bae T1A Hawks – in glorious black finish, I might add – were waiting to take off, and where was I? Right behind them, side-on by about 15m. If they had set take-off power at that moment, they would have rolled me over for sure, so I hurriedly reversed and held my breath. The thrust/ weight ratio for a Hawk is 0.65, delivering 5,700lbs of thrust – Wikipedia told me so. The RAF use Hawks for training pilots, as well as for the *Red Arrows* fleet. Don't be fooled that they are small fast-jet trainers. If I had stayed put behind them, I would have lived, but been traumatised. That would have meant hospital for my hearing alone, and bandages for everything else.

A peacefully-drifting plane

A friend of mine whom I will call 'Captain Custard', gave me strict instructions not to tell this next one to anybody, but I couldn't resist. Sorry Rich. He told me how he had controls of the ATR72 heading to Brussels one afternoon, while the captain was handling the radio messages. It goes something like this… "I had the aircraft profiled beautifully for an approach, but every couple of minutes inexplicably it would pitch upwards slightly. The autopilot was on so I wondered why it was happening. No problem I just pushed on the control column and it was fine. Each time I corrected it and the captain didn't seem to notice. He was staring out the window. After the third time, I checked the autopilot and somehow it was off. Neither of us had checked it, so I just pushed the button and it was on again. Oops!" Basically then, the plane wasn't even flying itself – it was peacefully drifting in the skies. Nice work, Captain Custard. That's why you're the professional.

I have watched many episodes of *Air Crash Investigation*, where disaster has occurred – not because of anything major usually – but more often from a sequence of tiny departures from routine, mistakes that should have been noticed and rectified.

One such episode focussed on an American Airlines flight to Cali, Colombia, in 1995, where the pilots veered off course so drastically that although they thought they were on approach to their destination, they were so far off that they actually flew into a mountain, killing most of the occupants on board. The main reason was they had become occupied with programming the flight computer to follow uncertain report points, and had accidentally deleted the ones they needed. They had ended up setting coordinates for Bogota, Columbia instead, and had ended up flying a course in a parallel valley. Because they had forgotten that they still had speed-brakes deployed (spoilers on the wings), by the time they realised they had to climb to avoid the mountain they were heading towards, they had insufficient power to accelerate out of danger.

Another one, perhaps more shocking is the story of 'ghost-flight' Eastern 401, a Tristar which crashed into the Everglades swamps in Florida. This was a chilling story, not just because of what happened, but what occurred after the crash, in other aircraft which used spare parts recovered from the crash site. The main point however is that the pilots became so fixated by a possible broken bulb in a landing-gear warning light, that they ignored the instruments which were telling them the autopilot was not on. They lost height so dramatically on that evening approach into Miami, that by the time they realised it, the heavy trijet had hit the swamps, and their transponder (ID) blip on the guiding-air traffic controller's screen, simply vanished. The flight engineer was climbing out of the 'hell-hole' (flight deck floor hatch) at the time of hitting the swamp. If the impact didn't kill them all, then it was either death by drowning or by alligators.

I recall sitting in the classroom on an Air 2000 *ab-initio* course during safety and emergency training, being shown a very grainy and very eighties VHS video: a *World in Action* reconstruction of a Saudia Tristar fire in August 1980. I wasn't the only one who sat very quietly during, and after, the showing. The three flight crew had made a tragic shambles of communicating with each other, and to the cabin crew, displaying no idea of how to decisively tackle an onboard fire. As they returned to Riyadh, the fire had spread from the aft cargo hold and into the cabin, causing chaos. Once they had landed, they should have come to as quick a stop as possible for an immediate evacuation to save as many lives as possible. They were however detained by ATC to wait for a royal flight to taxi ahead. Once the engines had stopped, several precious minutes later, the emergency services eventually gained access and found everyone dead on board from smoke inhalation. Horrifically, there were 38 bodies jammed into the flight deck which could seat five only.

That's an extreme example of flight crew not jelling, not being decisive and not knowing their routines properly. Routines are unavoidable. Predictable, sometimes tedious and, for me, as someone who would rather cut through red tape, they are necessary to provide boundaries, which once crossed can lead to danger. Let's face it they are dull, but necessary. How often do we have to endure them at work, say the right things, play the game, when all we're really thinking of is surfing, music, sex or fun. I sometimes look around me, wondering if others might be thinking similar things: if they are, then they're doing a grand job of disguising it. When I have had the chance to do something different or seize an opportunity, I have usually done it quickly and not thought of the consequences as you will see....

Miracles in the Middle East – out of the airline world awhile...

I belong to a couple of exclusive clubs. I am one of a limited number of people who have been lucky enough to fly as a passenger on Concorde (to New York JFK in Jan.1999). This was a lifetime's ambition for some people, so perhaps I treated it too lightly, being an airline employee at the time and only paying £410 for the privilege, one way. In case you're wondering, I returned on a regular jumbo in World Traveller class, and let's just say it was a totally different experience. Plus the de-icing took two hours pre-departure ex-JFK. I 'slept' badly across three seats, whereas on Concorde I was treated like a king. The supersonic CSD (chief steward) had taken an obvious shine to me, and it was he and one of the female C/As who had cleared with the captain that we could get a lift into Manhattan with them in the crew bus.

They had also laden me with extra goodies like *Sennheiser* headphones, *Pol Roger Cuvee Sir Winston Churchill 1986* Champagne and leather stationery packs. The rest of the NYC trip was short and predictable by comparison, except for a ten-minute helicopter trip above the city when the twin towers were still standing casting their shadows over Central Park.

The other club I belong to is, arguably, way more dramatic. I went to Iraq in July 2003 – and evidently returned alive. You might be thinking, "Why did you go?!" Well, you wouldn't be alone. (Three of us went to visit Mikey, a friend working for a relief organisation.) I kissed my mum goodnight and as she slept, I whispered: "Night, Ma. I won't see you for a week, because I'm going to fly out to Baghdad tomorrow, but I'll see you next Saturday." (I later found out from my dad that she had awoken the next morning and said, "Gino, I had a really strange dream, that Simon was going to Baghdad?!" Apparently, he could only reply in his Venetian accent: "Yes woman – it's true!") Thankfully they didn't try to stop me or call the airport, so I was free to sample 'English cake' ice-cream at 1am that night in Amman, Jordan – our transit point.

The 06:00 hotel departure time came around very quickly, as did our check-in the following morning, and we were bumped off the UN chartered flight (a twin turboprop King Air feeder-liner with about 22 seats) owing to weight restrictions and overbooking. The first miracle happened as I led the prayer in the departure lounge, using the airline lingo to appeal to our Maker: "Please

Lord, let there be no-shows and voluntary offloads – we need to get onto this flight. Thank you!"

Twenty minutes later Mikey, my friend who was our Iraq contact, was chaperoned into the airline office behind the check-in area, and a couple of minutes later came over to the three of us, beaming: "OK guys, better check in – we're on!" Airlines traditionally overbook flights to a 10% standard, based on the amount of no-shows. I worked out that here, there was a 70% no-show rate, as we took off with nine pax including the four of us. (God sometimes likes to exceed our expectations.)

Landing at *Sadaam International* was humbling and exciting for me, but nothing could prepare me for the dry oven-heat that baked me as soon as the aircraft doors were opened. The next five days left an indelible impression on me as I saw so many amazing things that the media just won't show you. I climbed up onto a tank to have my picture taken with the soldiers, faked a press conference for our cameras in the UNHQ, attended military press-briefings, participated in a meeting to discuss improvement to the GP/ medical practitioner system which would affect a million people and patrolled streets in the back of a U.S. 101st Airborne division 'Hummer'. I laughed with locals at my long shorts, ate Iraqi-style fast food, had a rifle trained on me by a US Army soldier atop an armoured vehicle, distributed medical supplies and encouraged the same Mike, who was based there in his role for a charity/NGO (non-governmental organisation). I saw first-hand how competent and well-organised the military are, visited the ruins of Babylon and took lots of 35mm photos too.

On day four, Bill – a fellow traveller – and I were in a taxi. The driver was telling us in broken English: "Sadaam good! George Bush – bad! Sadaam – we have water, electricity, money! George Bush – no water, no electricity, no money!!" This was as we were crossing through the suburbs, from a journalists' hotel to Mikey's place, and it dawned on Bill and me how precarious our situation was, especially had we chosen not to listen, but to argue back. There was more, but you'll have to wait for the sequel....

Miracle No.2 occurred during our ten-hour MPV journey back through the Iraqi desert motorway. We had been denied a free flight back on the UN plane, as this time there was nothing available, so we accepted our lot, paid $50 each and left Baghdad at sunrise, having piled into the black Mitsubishi. Our driver insisted on showing us how he could perform elaborate finger-clicking moves to Arabic music on the stereo, while his hands were off the wheel, at motorway speeds. I liked him straight away.

Four hours into the drive, Mikey turned around to us having translated the Arabic news on the radio. He simply said slowly and soberly: "Guys, it's a good job we weren't on that flight earlier. A platoon of American soldiers were ambushed and a few of them killed, in a rocket-propelled grenade attack on the Airport Road." (We would have been highly visible in a UN marked bus travelling on the Airport Road, had we been accepted onto that flight.) I will never know for sure if we would have been caught up in that, but I can honestly answer for the four of us, that we were very quiet for a while in that 4x4, and I for one know undeniably God had our backs. That reflective mood lasted until we crossed the border into Jordan, and into relative safety. Three weeks later, a terrorist drove a truck laden with explosives into the east wing of the UNHQ building that we had been in three or four times during our stay. It had the best canteen in the country.

Routines give you order and discipline, and promote safety. That's why flying, for example, is comparatively safe — it's so heavily regulated, ordered and procedure-based, that as long as you follow the rules, the chances of anything going wrong are minimised. You'll find this in your own organisation if you work for a medium/large employer, and even small ones are having to comply. It's just the world we live in. Everything seems to be micro-managed to the point of obsession, and I don't think technology helps the feeling that we are all being conditioned in a mechanical and intrusive way — usually deliberately. My point is that routines don't guarantee safety, and can only prepare you for so much....

What happens if your engines shut down in flight?
Eric Moody was a British Airways jumbo captain on a 1982 flight over Jakarta Indonesia. At LGW, I worked occasionally with his son, who was a pilot sharing a house with one of my best friends Demetrius — an affable Greek-Cypriot fellow. (Sometimes

Demetrius, another mate Jamie, and I would borrow his uniform jacket and would wear his long leather riding boots pretending we were Herr Flick in *Allo' Allo!*) The reason I mention this is that his father piloted a 747 across volcanic ash which closed down all four engines, one by one. Yes, at 38,000ft they lost all of their engine power. He made an infamous public address: "Ladies and gentlemen, this is your captain speaking. We have a small problem. All four engines have stopped. We are doing our damnedest to get them going again. I trust you are not in too much distress." You can imagine the mood in the cabin at that point. The flight crew managed to glide the aircraft through the ash cloud – (remember kinetic energy in your physics lessons?) – and miraculously reignited the engines before diverting to Jakarta.

I was on a flight to MXP (Malpensa, Milan) which involved a slightly longer turnaround than usual, so I nipped off to get some fresh air on the apron, do a walk-around of my own, watching all sorts of international airliners come and go, so at least I could say I had touched the ground in Italy. A little like the Pope, but my lips didn't kiss the tarmac – after all, you don't know where I've been.

Back on board, at breakfast in the forward cabin, the flight engineer, who resembled Noel Edmonds, was telling me how, if all our engines failed, a tiny propellor on the underside of the huge-bellied-beast could be dropped and enable us to glide for up to another 120 miles, while it attempted to restart engines. I thought he was winding me up, and then I remembered from my childhood aircraft magazines, it's known as a ram air turbine or RAT. I asked him what would happen beyond those 120 miles, and still no engine power. I won't tell you his answer. A few years later in 2001, a Canadian Air Transat A330 which had run out of fuel over the Atlantic diverted to the Azores, and the RAT was used to help it provide instrument power in the absence of engine-power. It was later to be known as 'The Azores Glider.'

TCAS, ceilings and a sex-offender caught...

There is a phenomenon called clear air turbulence or CAT which can occur at any moment and is often unpredictable, except when flying over mountain ranges or into warm fronts. Air moves in a snake-like motion commonly known as a jet-stream and turbulence is caused when slower moving air meets a faster moving jet-stream. A cloudless sky can suddenly throw up turbulence out of the blue. I was once operating a regular shuttle flight from LHR to Manchester (MAN) – a daytime scheduled run, so routine and quick, that you're barely in the cruise and it's time to start the descent. On a quick run with a tail wind, it could be a 27 minute flight. About ten minutes away from MAN, I popped into the Airbus flight deck to collect some cups and the captain had a nervous expression on his face as he turned around to me. "What's happened?" I said. "We've just had a TCAS – my first one in twenty years..." he replied. (TCAS stands for Traffic Collision Avoidance System, which detects other aircraft inside of your allotted space, and sounds a loud warning horn in the flight-deck should the 1,000ft separation between airliners be broken. Evasive manoeuvres often result immediately.) Suffice to say this ruined his day, as it blemishes a safe flying record even if it is not your fault, and he had some heavy-duty paperwork – an ASR or Air Safety Report – to fill out. I felt his pain.

In aviation, we often talk of an aircraft having a 'ceiling' - a maximum operating altitude or a maximum usable height at which an aircraft can operate. The ATR advanced turboprops I used to work on, could operate more efficiently at lower altitudes such as 20,000ft. The T-tailed RJ100 whisper-jets could fly no higher than 35,000ft, but tended to cruise a few thousand feet lower on the short hops to Europe or the Channel Islands. The 757 could stretch to 41,000ft on a Mediterranean 'there and back', whilst the larger wide-bodied jets such as the Tristar, Triple-Seven and 747-400 could fly up to a ceiling of around 42,000ft. There was something slightly mind-blowing about being in the flight deck of any of these magnificent aircraft, and watching the slight wobble of the analogue-needle altimeter touching the heady heights of 40,000ft and realising that only a couple of inches separated you from sub-Arctic temperatures of minus 50 degrees Celsius: now that's cold.

While in the airlines, I came across the fact that wings are tested to their maximum endurance in the factory. Take Airbus for example: a chief engineer I knew, who tested A340 landing gear, told me that the wings are effectively bent until they almost touch at a vertical, just to test their stress factors. Stop and think about that: *until they almost touch??!* My first time on the Boeing 777, I was a pap (singular of pax), flying off to Havana, Cuba to start a 300-mile bicycle ride across the island. Barely five or ten minutes up in the air, I looked out of the windows into the sunshine to marvel with slight alarm at the angle of the huge wings flexing upwards on this giant airliner. The official wingspan is 61m, while the angle known as the wing sweepback is 31 degrees.

Incidentally, I made the front page of the local paper in readiness for that Cuba-trip. They took a photo of me on my bicycle, in my uniform and dispatcher's cap, with a rather cute Golden Retriever puppy balanced across the handlebars. It was all going so well when I saw my face on the front page, until I looked at the nearby caption which was meant for a separate story. Placed for all to see, which appeared to link my photo to it, was the headline, "Sex offender caught." Oh dear, and pictured with a puppy too…the shame of it.

The worst collision in history

On 27 March 1977, a bomb threat carried out at the main airport on Las Palmas, Gran Canaria (LPA) meant that all flights were diverted to the smaller Los Rodeos Tenerife (TFN) airfield. That day will sadly be remembered for the worst aircraft collision in history, between two chartered jumbo jets belonging to KLM and Pan Am. Remember what I said about a sequence of minor events aligning to contribute to a major catastrophe? Well, this is exactly what happened on that day. It was the culmination of the diversions, lack of space to park multiple airliners on the apron, the use of one runway for taxiing ('back-taxiing'), commercial pressures, time, the taking on of a full fuel-load on the KLM jumbo, misinterpretation of ATC instructions, stress and, crucially, fog, that all ultimately led to the impact of two fully laden 747 jumbo jets.

The accident is largely attributed to the ego and impatience of the KLM captain (a poster celebrity and chief training pilot) not waiting for the internationally-accepted phrase, "Cleared for take-off." Even though the first officer was handling the radios, he was in a hurry, and he was definitely going. Five hundred and eighty-three people were killed, mainly because of his impulsiveness. Having watched the re-creations and read the transcripts of what happened on the day, it still makes me shudder. Impulsivity is dangerous. It can manifest itself by lack of forethought, acting on a whim, a disregard for personal safety or that of others, or even a lack of self-control. It turns out to be a disorder, unsurprisingly, a key feature of ADHD (Attention Deficit Hyperactivity Disorder). Do I have ADHD? Dunno, I've never stuck around long enough to answer the question....

Every time I boarded a flight, no matter how routine, the thought would cross my mind: "Could this be my last...?" So, dear passenger, and even dear crew member, I know how you might feel. When you look at hijackings of the past for example, they range from the infamous 1971 *D.B. Cooper* apparently parachuting away through the rear air-stairs of the Northwest-Orient 727-100, to the Air France 8969 (CDG-ALG-MAR) in 1994, where the A300 was stormed by French Special Forces at Marseilles who shot all the Algerian hijackers dead – no messing around. Somewhere in between you have a BOAC VC10 blown up at Beirut to prove a political point, an Ethiopian 767 cartwheeling into the Indian Ocean, because a hijacker couldn't be bothered to listen to the captain's advice about running out of fuel, and a couple of more recent events concerning pilots tragically taking an Egyptair 767 and a Germanwings A320 into their own hands. So why do they do it? Political motivation, religious conviction, poor mental health and sheer desperation are the top drivers – or KPIs (Key Performance Indicators) as the business-people among you may prefer to term them.

I often exhibited a similar single-minded determination when I used to take those unused mini-jam jars off C-class breakfast trays, to store in my fridge at home. It didn't make me a hijacker. It's just that they made excellent Christmas gifts. Did that make me a danger to society? Only if my brioche wasn't warmed. As you'll see next, there's only so much flying a man can take, and you can always sense when it's time for a change….

Chapter Five

Grounded

Girls can break your heart. Even a singer in the 1980s, unfortunately called Randy, penned a song about girls being dangerous. So, not wanting to fly anymore, having had enough of the area, having achieved all he thought he could, coupled to the fact he didn't get the girl, a certain reluctant air steward hung up his wings and headed for home, or at least a regional airport nearby which claimed to be truly 'international'. "Wurzel International", as a comical pilot, Captain Dann once remarked.

Set in the gently rolling hills of the West country, Lulsgate was a village on the outskirts of Bristol, with a pub, another pub, a B&B and a cattle grid. It was about as international as the retired red-faced local farmer who had been propping up the bar since first sneaking a pint of rough cider as a 14 year-old. The sole terminal building seemed to have been built in the late sixties or early seventies, and exuded a kind of dated charm – a throwback to the days of black-and-white TV sets or flower-patterned brown curtains. The control tower was accessed via some stairs on the first floor, next to the airline offices and the cafe/restaurant, and sat perched on top of the terminal. You could even go upstairs to watch aircraft come and go whilst having a hot chocolate, a coffee or, if things were really that bad, a double brandy with a malt whisky chaser. The whole building had a sense of well-worn cosiness that was diametrically opposed to the ostentatious and soulless glass cavern that was to be the 'new' airport terminal the following year.

Blown away...

I sometimes used to go down to the 'old' airport with my trusty airband radio in the days before joining the industry, just to watch the few aircraft come and go, sometimes alone, but more often with friends. One day, when the traffic lights held up the cars to allow for a departing Airbus, we seized our chance. Five reprobates – boys and girls – suddenly appeared from behind a hedge, and ran towards the fence directly behind the runway threshold. Clinging on tightly to each other and the fence posts, we waited 30 seconds for the glorious event. We were 50m behind our target and were ill-prepared for what happened next. The Airtours A320 with 180 pax onboard opened up to full take-off power with a deafening roar, converting the drizzle into painful darts, and the severe jet blast blew two girls off the fence. We all clung on to each other for precious life, screaming inaudibly from delicious adrenaline, coughing out the kerosene fumes and shaking. Once the Airbus had disappeared into the low cloud base, the road re-opened and we laughed at our new bouffant hairstyles. The cows and sheep were used to the noise, whereas we were townies. What had I learnt from this? *That* was the reason they stopped the traffic. I'd do it all again tomorrow.

On hearing I was to join this airline, my friend Nigel had helpfully sent me the local newspaper's recent front page. There, in close-up and resplendent in full technicolor, was the startling image of a forlorn crashed airliner whose landing gear had collapsed at PLH (Plymouth). Underneath the photo, he had written the heart warming words: "Welcome to Brymon Airways, Simon!" Brymon, a wholly-owned subsidiary of BA, was one of the main scheduled operators out of Lulsgate, alongside BMI, KLM, Sabena, Aer Lingus, Air France and Jersey European. The charters had a base here too: Air 2000, Airtours and Britannia. The airport became busier in the summer with the appearances of Royal (Canada), Spanair, Aegean and others….

This could probably have been any other regional airport around the country. This one however had a major difference which was to be its downfall until someone wisely considered investing in a Category Three all-weather ILS (Instrument Landing System). The airport was prone to fog or, as known in this business, 'being fogged-out'. This meant that in fog, the runway was invisible, so that even the larger Airbus A320s were sometimes diverted to Exeter (EXT) or Cardiff (CWL). What was not widely known was the history of this airfield: apparently, the RAF used it as a test-bed in the Second World War, specifically for dropping bombs in fog. So, it was an obvious choice of location to construct an 'international airport'.

A Ford Fiesta with a flashing light on top

However, the young man, now in his late 20s needed a new challenge, and this change suited him. From one BA operator to another, the switch was made painlessly. He didn't get the Duty Manager-role, so he settled for a more junior customer service agent role, which involved check-in, departure gate and meeting arrivals on a coach. He hadn't calculated the startling drop in salary properly, but made the jump anyway. When the opportunity came up about three months in to work outside with aeroplanes, he seized it and made it his own role until it fitted him like a well-worn glove. He had been advised that if he worked outside his career path would lead to Station Controller, while inside he would probably end up as a Duty Manager. The reluctant air steward chose the outside option because that was where the action was, and was given a radio and a Ford Fiesta with a flashing light on top; he had made it – this was the pinnacle of his career to date.

Dispatch meant you could interact with the broadest range of personnel: flight and cabin crew, baggage-handlers, engineers, aircraft refuelers, caterers, marshallers, gate-staff, station-controllers, coach drivers, airfield safety unit – in fact anyone who dared venture outside into fresh country air and within the vicinity of a wing-tip. The only people you didn't dare to go near were the toilet-service guys in their 'special' truck. On one occasion, they didn't clear up a 'spillage' properly and left the fire appliance to do it properly with a high-pressure hose. The reluctant air steward only just made it to the Fiesta door in time, and the fire-fighters definitely had grins on their faces....

What I loved best about my job as an aircraft dispatcher, was the camaraderie: the sheer number of people involved in getting even a relatively small airliner away safely and on time meant that I got to know a lot of people in my time working outside. My favourite team was the engineers as they always seemed to have a glint in their eyes as if waiting for the next prank, while their humour could be as dirty as the oil stains on their white overalls. *Andy-avionics* would occasionally catch my eye when a particularly attractive girl was about to board the aircraft off the coach and both of us were useless at keeping ourselves composed. *Keith-engines* and *Ian-supervisor* were always buoyant characters with both dry wit and infectious giggles; it was their boots that could be seen jumping up and down, crunching a spillage of ice cubes from the rear galley door. Ian also told me his vasectomy didn't hurt, and I took note of this for the future. *The Welsh Boys* were certainly crude, but knew how to keep each other going during a long and painful aircraft repair. A fair proportion of them had come from the RAF and were experienced in many ways, including work and world-travel. Grown men with a boyish sense of good-humour and unspoken loyalty to each other.

There was a captain who shared my first name, was also a drummer and who affectionately called me 'numpty' – at least I think it was affectionately. Sometimes he would clock me outside, from his seat in the flight-deck, and we would see how we could give each other the middle finger in discreet and inventive ways without any of the joining/ disembarking pax knowing. The challenge was not to smile, and it made our days go by a little quicker. I was younger then.

The coach drivers were all a quirky bunch too and ended up sharing our ground radio frequency which usually resulted in reprimands such as: *"Proper radio procedures please,"* or *"May I remind colleagues that this is an open radio channel."* I am not saying by any means that it felt like a family – after all work is work, home is home, etc, but it helps enormously if, when you go to work, you can actually enjoy the company of most of your colleagues. The airline field attracts mainly open characters – those with good interpersonal skills (sounds like a CV) or are simply able to get on with others in a team, without any drama. Men especially need this camaraderie, as we are not so great at shopping trips or coffee with the girls. We need something more.....such as power-drills, fast bikes and sometimes even that *Nivea* after-shave balm stuff that gives your face a rare treat.

Technicalities of dispatch

Brymon's fleet was made up of Dash 8 -300 aircraft which were small 50-seaters but surprisingly sophisticated, containing all the usual *Honeywell* flight management systems, advanced glass cockpit suite, quiet cabin technology and even two tea-drinkers in the front. Day to day, the role of dispatch was pretty straightforward: to co-ordinate the safe turnaround of an aircraft within a tight timeframe, ensuring it was correctly loaded, adequately fuelled and accompanied by all supporting documentation, including the official load-sheet, before being signed off by the dispatcher and pilots as ready to go. (The equivalent title which means the same thing in other airlines is 'turnaround manager/co-ordinator'.) Basically, when a Dash 8 aircraft was scheduled to depart, you had 25 minutes to ensure it rolled off-chocks (wooden blocks) or off-stand. The doors had to be closed at 'minus three' (minutes) to allow for engine start and 'a minus-three closure' would count as an on-time close. (For larger aircraft, the turnaround time was extended to one-and-a-half hours to two hours.)

Within that Dash 8 time-frame of 22 minutes, pax had to be disembarked, aircraft had to be re-catered, toilet-serviced, unloaded/loaded, refuelled, tech log checked by engineers for any fixes needed, and new pax on. A crew change might slow things down, but the dispatcher was clock-watching and writing times in on a dispatch card to record the events. The baggage loaders would give me a 'Bingo-card' which was a sheet or more of A4, covered in baggage stickers, ripped off each piece of luggage, as it was stowed in the A/C hold. The eyes of experience would quickly tell you if a rogue bag had been loaded, as you rapidly scanned the text of each sheet. It often happened: a bag meant for CDG (Paris) would end up on an earlier CDG flight, separated from its owner and instantaneously becoming a security risk. This was in the 12 year period following the downing of Pan Am 103 over Lockerbie, and, ever since, bags have since had to be strictly matched to their owners.

Weight and balance: my name is Clarence...

Dispatch involves a high element of 'load control' and 'weight and balance' procedures. One key element was the setting of the elevator trim, in the tail section– the panels that give the aircraft lift. On the Dash 8, as with most airliners, this was a pair of round hand-turned wheels at the central console next to the pilots' seats. Get the trim calculation correct, and the aircraft could rotate without fear of a 'tail-strike' (a scraping of the rear underside fuselage at the point of lifting off the runway). It happens once in a while, even to the big boys like jumbos, and was a secret fear of mine that I might one day have to visit. On a smaller aircraft such as the ATR or the Dash 8, you had to be aware of weight distribution in the forward and rear cargo holds, centre of gravity for trim purposes and amount of fuel on-board. You start off with a calculation called a 'zero fuel weight', add on your passenger and cargo load, fuel itself and expected burn, finishing up with landing weight at your destination. That landing weight is a precisely calculated sum and has to be within the margins of the manufacturer's approved landing weight, otherwise you have to dump fuel, and that's a waste, except in an emergency of course.

Occasionally, just as with larger airliners, you may have to move passengers around to different seats. Would this make a difference to the weight distribution? Of course. For example, R'n'B star Aaliyah's Cessna 402 crashed in the Caribbean in 2001 because of severe overloading, even before the nine occupants actually entered the equation. It turned out that this was a fatal mix of ego-pressure and the pilot's inability to handle the situation. The weights we used to calculate at Brymon were standard BA-issued: 88 kilos for a man and his baggage, 70 kilos for a woman, and 35 kilos for a child. Babies were zero kilos, understandably. Fuel can be pumped around an airliner into different tanks to distribute the weight evenly during flight, and these systems have been around for decades. (On early jet airliners, the flight engineer or 'third pilot' would have been largely responsible for overseeing this.) The above was exactly the same as any larger aircraft which departs from any major hub around the world. Some of the Dashes had fuel gauges in pounds (lbs), while most of them were in kilos, so if I went on to check how much fuel was already onboard, ahead of flight crew, I had to be certain which denomination it was in – and I don't mean Baptist. Get this bit wrong, and it could end up being a repetition of a 1983 Air Canada Boeing 767 which ran out of fuel at 41,000ft. (Don't worry – they landed that plane fine using the captain's glider knowledge.) Always wise, therefore, to double-check everything....

One day I had a Dash all ready to push and start, but had a message from Station Control to hold it for a few 'rush bags' (mislaid baggage to be reunited with their owners) which would of course alter the weight and balance. I spoke to the captain via the headphones, plugging them into the base of the nose area and asked him if he wanted a new load-sheet (see explanation below.) He told me in ultra-relaxed Dutch tones: "Hey, don't worry about it, these aircraft are always a little nose-heavy. I'm happy to depart. See ya!" He wasn't troubled by an extra 50kg in the rear. His name was 'Clarence', and for the record, anyone who shares a name with a famous cross-eyed lion, is always OK in my book. Back to the story....

A load of ballast

Imagine the load-sheet's been produced by Station Control, with all the weights, aircraft details, loads and trim details all correct, then at the aircraft side someone needs to change something – usually with everyone on board at about four minutes before doors closed time. The LMC feature allowed you to manually adjust up to 200kgs weight up/down on the Dash 8, in the section unsurprisingly marked 'Last minute change'. You could add 'engineering spares 175kg' or 'minus 1 male, 1 bag 88kg, 1 female 70 kg ABZ' (Aberdeen).

Or, if you had forgotten to add ballast in the hold (usually a handful of sand bags at about 25kgs each), you could do so at this stage. Ballast? Why do you need that?! It's needed to keep the aircraft in trim so it can take off. As Charlie, one of my favourite captains reminded me discreetly from the observers seat, while line-checking the two pilots in front when we were ready to go one morning: "We'd look a bit silly waiting to go at the end of the runway without it in the hold!" Point taken, I worked quickly to get it loaded, and off they went with a couple of waves. Naughty dispatcher trying to cut corners.

The new Embraer Brazilian-made jet fleet soon came to BRS and with it a certain amount of fawning over, especially by managers. These slimline jets looked like mini-Concordes in a way, and had a similarly-cramped cabin, but with less overall performance, an awful white-noise roar from the auxiliary power unit (APU), and, laughably could only be kept in trim for take off by permanently keeping 200 kgs of sand bags in the rear hold to maintain the centre of gravity. Perhaps Embraer should have sold them with the sacks too?

The spring arrived and, with it, came warmer weather, so the tie could be dispensed with unless there was a manager floating around. There were two main shift patterns: an early start at 05:45 and a late start at 13:00 approximately. The first wave of flights from BRS departed daily from 07:25 to 08:55, ranging from EDI (Edinburgh) or NCL (Newcastle)/ABZ (Aberdeen) to the transit flight known as the 'Plymouth/ Jersey/ Paris' (PLH/ JER/CDG). The pair of dispatchers were allotted two each at a time, often seen racing from one set of steps to another if they were departing at the same time. If someone was ill, then unless help came from inside the terminal, it was not uncommon for one of us to send four away simultaneously carrying four different sets of paperwork while the radio was issuing constant updates and demands. The worst shifts were at the weekends: a 12-hour Saturday and a 12-hour Sunday, followed by an early on the Monday. As the airfield was traditionally quieter, it was a struggle to find things to do, so it was wash the dispatch car, drink yet more tea or hide somewhere for a snooze.

Foraging: This aspect of the afternoon shift was discovered late-on in my career, but it was possible to raid the larders of an aircraft free of flight personnel, during that unknown time period before the catering truck arrived to collect the used trolleys and swap over for brand new ones ready for the next flight rotation. All you had to do was walk boldly to the rear galley, break the pointless plastic seals of the food trolley and check for any intact leftovers, such as bread rolls, cheese, sausages, packets of biscuits or chocolate. Job done, new seal applied and foraging complete. Bar trolleys were a 'no-no'. They could be traced, owing to numbered pink seals and paperwork, plus it would have been instant dismissal so barely worth it, besides there were other ways of keeping your car mini-bar stocked…you just had to know the right cabin crew. They usually had shockingly open stories to relay and a slightly wild look in their eyes. Mine's two Gordon's, and a Jamesons please.

Running late

Tight flight connections were to be expected at a regional base, but here was demonstrated the value of contingency. If you were making a long journey by car, with a ferry to catch at the other end, hopefully you would give yourself a little buffer of time to allow for traffic jams or motorway breaks to spare yourself the stress of missing the sailing. Why then, did pax leave so little time for themselves to connect with another departure onwards? I saw it time and time again: for example, an I/B Dash coming in from say CDG at 15:30 touchdown STA (scheduled time of arrival) with four pax transferring onto the EDI, which was to leave BRS at 16:00. All it takes is for a very minor delay of say, a quarter of an hour, for the pax to not stand a chance of making their EDI in time, taking into account landing, taxiing onto stand, baggage retrieval if not through-checked and making it by coach onto the next A/C. I think these days pax are wise to it; if the plane is going at 16:00 STD, then the plane is going with or without you, as Bono once sang. If there are enough onward connecting pax, then I have seen planes held for them, but the decision to do so lies with Ops and it's usually commercially biased.

Another scenario I have seen many times, is a pap attempting a late check-in, but the departing A/C is still on the ground waiting to go. The natural reaction for anyone in this situation is: "Why can't I just get on, it hasn't left yet?!" Check-in and gate-staff will apologise, but this just isn't procedure. If everyone has checked in, the gate has closed and all are on board, the aircraft is presumed to be in a 'ready to depart' phase, with the final checks being made pre-engines-start. To undo all that would not only set a precedent for which there is no value, but to further delay an aircraft's departure by even a minute or two costs money as well as affecting departure statistics, and makes a mockery of all those who have managed to get there on time themselves. If this sounds harsh, I write as one who has missed planes – it's just the system and sometimes it's easier and less stressful to go along with it. Like the guy on an ABZ departure who the girls were worried about. Apparently, he had been drinking heavily in the lounge and was making comments to the crew once seated onboard, to the extent that they spoke to me in the galley and asked me to offload him. At the time I hated any form of confrontation, but I spoke quickly to the captain who gave me his blessing to do so, and I calmly walked up to the business man concerned and asked him to follow me. No protest, no argument, no scenes and no punches, he just followed me off the Dash, down the steps and into the Fiesta, where I drove him back to the terminal explaining that the crew weren't happy to take him on this evening's flight. Unbelievably, he accepted it and I left him to find himself another way of getting to his destination. I had a back-up plan which involved Graham the captain, who was a well-built rugby player. Luckily for the pap, I didn't need to resort to that one.

When there's precious little time to play with, dispatchers could do without duplication of numbers. One sunny Sunday afternoon, I had managed to close doors on-time on my two Dashes, but my colleague Sam was having a problem. I asked if I could help, but she declined: "It's already picked up an hour's delay and I'm now one passenger over- I've got to tell the captain the bad news..." I grimaced when she told me who it was: a guy with a reputation for being a stress-head, and watched her disappear up the steps into the flight deck. I counted to three, and waited for the captain's *Homer Simpson* scream, which was audible outside as well as inside the cabin. The engineers laughed and shook their heads. Most of the time, even if the headcount revealed one or even two extra persons onboard, it was usually a check-in error with a duplicated boarding pass. Sometimes a pap for a later flight would have been mistakenly checked in for an earlier flight and made it onboard. Just like with the fuel and baggage, the dispatcher's job, would be to account for TOB (total on board). Sometimes this could manifest itself in tensions between personnel so that you felt you were battling each other rather than working together for a common solution.

I had a full GLA ready for an 07:30 departure one morning with three pax named 'Smith' onboard. It's a common name, but only two 'Smiths' were supposed to be on this flight. To cut a long story short, and not wanting to perform a full baggage I.D. (everybody disembarks and, one by one, identifies their unloaded hold baggage outside before returning to their seats) I had to make a decision as a half-hour delay causes a knock-on to the schedule. After doing all the radioing and running about that I could, I decided that all onboard were good to go and that it was a check-in error. As the red anti-collision lights slowly flashed and the turboprop rolled off stand, the captain gave us the usual wave, whilst I reviewed the paperwork in the car. The blame-game started, but not before a few colleagues had metaphorically dug in the knives at my decision to let the aircraft go, with just minimal information and self-belief. Only one colleague stood up for me and confirmation came within a few minutes that it had indeed been a mistake at check-in, and a flight-change for the third 'Smith'. I was disappointed that my experience counted for so little…. I remained unusually quiet for the remainder of the shift. Watch the quiet ones.

"Don't you miss flying…?"

You might be thinking to yourself, "Didn't you miss flying and actually going somewhere?" At this juncture, I didn't. I certainly didn't want to fly for this company as I would have had to start off as a junior C/A again, on very short routes with little challenge for me. I had just done all this, and far more, at the second largest airport in the UK. I did notice among only a couple of regional

C/As an attitude of 'you're only ground-staff', and a brusqueness with it. One C/A who shall remain nameless used to strike terror into the hearts of anyone in her vicinity, owing to her deportment, her no-nonsense outlook and her stern face. One morning, about five of us were sat at the front of the Dash chatting, when an engineer called out from the bottom of the steps: "Quick! Sally *****'s coming!" You have never seen five grown men abandon ship so quickly: it was a textbook evacuation to be proud of. The vast majority of cabin crew and pilots too, were very friendly and easy to work alongside, especially when they knew that you had 'flown before'. A few girls would not only make you a coffee on turnarounds, but would also have taken the trouble to foil wrap a sandwich or snack they had ear-marked for you, knowing that you were going to greet their aircraft on return later in the day. Very touching. (I noted none of the boys ever made me anything special, and for that I was grateful.)

Some C/As would eventually end up as cabin crew for larger airlines like BA, Emirates or Virgin Atlantic out of larger bases, losing the intimacy of being known and being swallowed up into a large international organisation, with a six digit staff number. Some would stay and see it out before leaving for a different career. Some would get pregnant, like Michelle…. Carmel, an Irish C/A who was on secondment to a customer service role, asked me how I was getting on one day. I told her about how hard it was to get some printing done in the crew-room, as Michelle was very territorial about use of 'her' photocopier. Quick as a flash, Carmel pointed to her own navel and replied: "Well, she wasn't very territorial *down there*, was she?!!" I had to agree. Perhaps we should choose our 'territories' more carefully: maybe Carmel had tried to use Michelle's printer too?

When the winter came, it brought along the North wind that you read about in children's books. That wind would blow an unimpeded course straight across the airfield and when the temperature dropped to freezing, you would struggle to stay standing in its path. The snow followed, and, with limited resources to cope with natural elements (which meant only one de-icer vehicle for the whole airfield), the airport would shut down for flight-operations. We would pack people onto coaches for LHR or LGW where the promise of an alternative flight would mean an extra few hours journeying, in the hope that the two main airports were still active, by the time the pax arrived to catch their onward flights.

Out in the late December snow one evening, a Dash 8 was preparing for departure, with about twenty pax onboard strapped in, and ready to go. Outside however, the sole snowplough for the airport was driving up and down Runway 2-7 Left, unsuccessfully clearing the snowfall. As fast as it cleared the snow from the tarmac, just as much – if not more – came in behind it. This plane sadly, was going nowhere and neither I, nor Trevor, the captain would even think of letting it go either. I think I made a PA to the pax on behalf of the cabin crew, saying something about doing everything in our power to make the flight happen, but not wanting to compromise safety. The blizzards outside the open cabin door almost whited out the dark skies and this aircraft would surely have ended up as a statistic, if it had even managed to climb out of BRS at all. The Christmas card backdrop belied the underlying danger.

Comedy airport

If you're thinking to yourself that 'regional' might mean sensible, then think again. I was signing off the load sheet for a PLH departure one morning, when the captain turned to me in a posh voice and asked: "Do you like sheep?" An innocent, but loaded, question. I paused for a moment and delivered my balanced reply: "Sometimes." Turning to his F/O, the captain said: "It's alright Nigel – he's one of us!" I left the flight deck smiling, closed the door and felt happy to be a member of a new club I knew absolutely nothing about.

Another time, I was in Station Control's (SC) building, a prefab bolted onto the hangar, and was relayed this story by one of the tech guys. SC receive a radio call from an inbound Paris, halfway home…

"Station Control, Bristol: Brymon 4031".

"Brymon 4031– go ahead…".

"Er, we seem to be using more fuel than usual, and the aircraft seems to be dragging – can you advise? Over…".

Engineer: "Have you checked your landing gear is up?"

Long pause on the radio, and a quiet reply from 4031: "Er… thanks…".

One morning I was signing off a Dash to leave for PLH, when Alyson, the No.1 at the main entrance door, motioned for me to look at the galley entrance down the back. Standing there out of pax sight with arms folded and at an angle indicating confidence, was her No.2, Gareth. He had wrapped an entire toilet roll around his face and head, in a conical shape, saving two holes for his eyes and resembled a KKK member gone more wayward. (I have nothing but contempt for that organisation, so saw Gareth's version as parody.) I was impressed at his ingenuity, and mildly upset that I hadn't thought of it first. I'm sure I saw his photo in a Guinness Book of World records a couple of years ago as one of their staff, wearing a striped jacket. I'm certain too, that he would have found a way of securing an unusual world record himself, probably involving *Andrex*.

Meanwhile, inside the terminal, I had befriended Nick, a Greek-Cypriot wide-boy who ran the Avis Rent-a-Car kiosk. He had a liking for fast cars and even faster girls, and would occasionally discreetly pull out a bottle of Jack Daniels from under the counter, if I supplied the cans of Coke. It made the afternoon shifts feel more relaxed, and I felt that the quality of late-shift work

I delivered after these visits to 'Nicos Avis Taverna', was somewhat superior – especially after the third shot. (This was the same Nicos, whom while out on a Saturday night, found himself in the middle of an argument involving two of his lady friends and a taxi driver, which was spilling out into a street brawl. He suddenly flashed his police 'badge', holding it high, announcing: "Detective Constable Nick M*******, Avon and Somerset Police, the situation's under control. Ladies – please follow me…!" Everyone backed down and they all quickly got away in another taxi. (Nicos' badge turned out to be an Avon & Somerset Police Constabulary diary. It was a truly Greek-Cypriot piece of audacity.) More Halloumi, anyone?

Outside on the ramp, I would often become bored, and so my animal disguises would help me through the day. My two plastic masks often came out to play. I was one day informed by my manager that they had received reports from Servisair personnel, that "a cow" had been seen driving the Fiesta around the Jaguar-painted Ryanair and associated aircraft, and did I know anything about it? I took it as a compliment and stopped for a graze every now and then. Moo!

When the new terminal was about to be opened, I was invited to the proceedings but decided I had met enough famous people and was not hungry to stand on show in my full uniform to meet the Princess Royal. At T-minus four days, I was asked if I was looking forward to the big day, and casually declared that I was not really interested, but thanks anyway. My supervisor looked horrified when I said I had thrown the invitation on the fire. "Simon, you were one of the chosen few who had been vetted by Buckingham Palace!" Try as I might, I couldn't find even a shred of the invitation and instead endured 'a bad day on the ramp' with a bad-tempered station controller and an aircraft which suffered a three-hour delay. Not too sensible on that occasion.

Nor was I acting too cleverly when asked to take an UNMIN (unaccompanied minor) to the awaiting Paris flight about 500m away; he looked kind of quiet and introverted (remember: always watch the quiet ones), so I said to him in a low voice: "Wanna see some handbrake skids?!" He came alive: "Yeah!" As I approached G-YS, the awaiting Dash 8, I misjudged my third and final skid, which brought me to within a metre of the base of the steps and a near-coronary at the thought of writing off a £10m aircraft. As I shuddered, he asked if we could do it again. With my heart still in my mouth I declined his well-meant request and drove back very slowly from Yankee Sierra....That happened to be the day when I nearly didn't bother coming into work because of the snowfall.

It was a week before Christmas, and the whole airfield was at a standstill with just three aircraft standing on the ramp, and none of them belonging to our airline. Meanwhile, pax were still turning up for their booked flights which meant by midday, which is when I had dropped my UNMIN off at G-YS, there were seven times the normal amount of waiting pax in the departure lounge. The backlog was slowly whittled down over the course of the day and into the evening, with some flights being cancelled, as the airfield was not much more than an ice-rink. It was tiring and mentally demanding to keep going. In any delay situation pax seem to think that if ground staff don't appear to be flustered or in any particular hurry, then we don't care and are actually part of the problem. The reverse is true: adversity creates a knock-on effect: re-bookings, cancellations, aircraft changes, bad feeling, headaches and anxiety of the worst kind. It's the last thing airport workers would want because it causes supreme stress for both sides, and, quite frankly, screws up an operation for airline and airport alike, not to mention the pax, onward connections and people waiting at the other end.

I recall later that evening letting off steam in the otherwise empty terminal with a handful of colleagues as we were sitting on a baggage belt at the check-in desks. In wandered a crew who had just landed and completed their day. The captain called me over and said: "Simon, don't you think it's inappropriate that you're all sitting down- after all the bad weather today?!" The poor chap was completely oblivious of how much work had gone on behind the scenes to get about 14 flight loads of pax organised and away on their respective journeys, while he and his crew had done a there-and-back – one return plane journey. I told him straight that after a horrendous day, this was the first time we had sat down, and he should have been here to witness the chaos of the previous ten hours. I was pretty polite about it, but he got the message. Attitudes like his do little to dispel a 'them and us' situation.

The following summer, a call from Station Control came for me to meet an aircraft with a special load. With reverence, the Servisair baggage-loaders pulled the tiny white coffin out of the Dash 8's rear hold, and loaded it carefully onto a flat-bed lorry in silence. I had a sudden flashback to my Faro flight as a 12 year-old. The parents watched in tears, holding each other tightly. I had to turn away towards the afternoon sun. That was a hard moment. Among the work and occasional frivolity, there were reminders of your own mortality, and the sadness of the world around you. The reluctant air steward needed to address this imbalance, and craved an adventure that was beyond the parameters of the airline world, so naturally, he would need to take a plane journey to the Caribbean again, and abandon the industry for a long while. This was to involve putting others first, by building an orphanage. He was to end up labouring, cementing and plumbing as part of a team of Tearfund volunteers. You could indeed say he was at long last grounded in every sense of the word....

Chapter Six

Passenger Psychology

You've bought your e-ticket, you've made the long journey to the airport, perhaps having had to get there in the middle of the night just to avoid any chance of being late, you've checked in at last and you're still feeling tense. It doesn't matter that you've done this many times before, as each time is different. The butterflies in your stomach won't go away and you are gently perspiring, so you take your bags with you to the toilets to freshen up. When you get back, someone else has taken your seat: "Oh well, it's a busy airport and it has to be expected. Why is there a brand new Ferrari right in the middle of the concourse – and how did they get it there?! How much eau de parfum does that store sell every hour? When are they going to announce my gate on the screen? What if I miss my flight? Those caps they're wearing – are they Jewish? What is that woman thinking of – wearing a skirt like that with *those* legs?! That baby looks so cute, asleep in her pushchair. What was that announcement?! Have I missed something? I've been sitting here for nearly 30 minutes. It's really loud here...That couple look a strange combination...I wouldn't have put them together. How many bags does she need?! I had a jacket just like that...That poor man in the wheelchair – he just can't get past everyone...wish I could help. Have they called my gate yet? Have I got my passport and boarding pass? Good, it's in that pocket, safe. I don't trust anyone here. Those Middle Eastern-looking guys – are they staring at me? I can't believe they took my toiletries away from me at security! I'm hardly a risk! My phone…where is it?!"

Stress and imaginations. It's not surprising that – once a passenger actually makes it to the departure gate, to have his boarding pass swallowed at the machine or have his/her mobile-phone checked – he or she is a bundle of nerves, despite looking cheerful on the outside. It's as if the airport has put so many automated hurdles to cross in your way to catch you out, before you even get close to an aircraft door. By the time a passenger is walking down the angled jetty, he/she is now going at a faster pace with trolley bag wheels rippling on the floor until a small funnel of queue builds up at the aircraft entrance: the finish line with a welcome sight – a doorway with a smiling, perhaps attractive uniformed member of staff to usher you in. Once through, the boarding music calms you a little, as you take in the cabin atmosphere and press your way down the slender aisle to locate your seat by looking at the numbers above each row. Once you've stretched high to push your cabin bags into the overhead locker, you can now squeeze into your ECY (economy) seat and sit down, breathing a few sighs. Looking out of the window, you can see a flurry of activity from men and the occasional woman in Hi Viz waistcoats, holding radios, pieces of paper, driving all sorts of trucks and weird vehicles with safety rails, conveyor belts and,

crucially, amber flashing-beacons. Turning your head inwards
again, you resume people-watching, observing the stress some
people visibly have – usually families with young children – the
nonchalance of the suited executive and the giggles from the young
couple carrying backpacks. You start to feel a little more... human.

Boarding time

For us professionals who are doing our jobs, it is sometimes hard to
understand the stresses of pax during the two hours or so leading
up tot the flight and the planning involved in even getting as far as
the airport terminal itself. When we greet you, it's both a welcome
and an analysis of several things: your boarding pass certainly for
obvious reasons, your physique/ travel status (if a sole traveller,
could we use you as an ABP – able-bodied person – in case of
evacuation?), but also your character and anything that might
suggest trouble. Rudeness is picked up on immediately, and any
signs of a bad attitude, aggression or even danger are flagged
mentally at that point. The commander is informed in the flight
deck pre-departure of anything – no matter how slight – that could
threaten the safety of the flight. This occasionally includes things
on the airframe (body of the aircraft) that a pax has spotted during
boarding, and there have been many occasions when the F/O has
come into the cabin to take a look for himself. We do use pax
knowledge, or just plain eyesight, and most things turn out to be

fine. It's the one occasion when you don't take it seriously that could be that time....

Nicki, my trainer at Air 2000 told us a story about a guy who made a 'comic' throwaway comment about having a bomb in his suitcase while boarding a holiday flight. Even though it was obvious he didn't mean it, she looked at him and replied, "You're really going to wish you hadn't said that, sir..." The police were called, the guy taken off and questioned and the baggage offloaded for 233 pax, delaying the flight for about three hours. That's how you make yourself the most unpopular person on a plane. That, and attempting any act which would interfere with the safety of an A/C, like Richard Reid, *'the Shoe-bomber'* on an American Airlines (AA) CDG (Paris) to MIA (Miami) in 2001. Next time you're on a plane, I can bet you find yourself studying your fellow pax, just in case....Even in my charter days, we were often astounded at how many passengers would leave their brains at home, before stepping on-board. Something seemed to happen to certain characters, once they stepped over the threshold from jetty to blue carpet, which involved either assuming a new personality or ditching all reason and becoming irrational. Families with young children I felt for, as it can be hard enough to look after yourself, let alone a couple of little people with their own wills and intentions.

The premium wing

The most-demanding – and sometimes repulsive – type of people often belonged to the premium wing of the airlines' business core. Simply put, a business customer/ member of any executive club/ frequent flyer or Club/ First Class passenger. Please don't think in writing this, I include everyone I have ever had the pleasure of flying in these brackets. By a long way, these customers were mainly genteel, respectful and good-natured. However, it must be said that I have witnessed the biggest tantrums and nit-picking behaviour from among this class of customer. There was the sarcastic know-it-all in One-Alpha to St.Petersburg/Leningrad (LED): "Oh dear, British Airways aren't doing very well today, are you?" (The poor dear was obviously unhappy before he boarded. Also he didn't get his first choice of meal and landing cards hadn't been loaded.) I retorted with: "Well, I make that just two things that have 'gone wrong' out of a possible thousand, so I'd say we are doing pretty well today actually!" The F/O congratulated me for standing our ground.

There were numerous examples of comments on 'delays' – my idea of a delay is seven hours, not 40 minutes, even though that is, of course, a delay. There was the gentleman who had been 'involuntarily downgraded' from Club World, who came to the mid-galley to vent, but I knew all about him before he opened his mouth. "Do you always refer to people who sit in Economy as 'down the back'?" He had overheard me talking to a colleague and assumed that I was being derogatory, but I assured him it was just an expression. No matter what I offered it was never going to be good enough, and he just wanted to get it out of his system. Yet another frequent flyer moaned for a nearly-unbroken three hours en route to LHR, during a night flight from Africa, which landed at about 05.30. He spoke loudly on disembarking that he would be switching to Virgin (Atlantic) from then on. I thought to myself: "You think Virgin don't have any problems?!" The experience you have on a given day depends on so many variables, ranging from how your journey went to get to the airport, the speed and friendliness of check-in, to the quality of the flight itself. It's all very subjective, and it takes very little to rock the boat, as you might see next....

A full jumbo jet – and he just fancied a moan...

One of my most memorable interactions was with a Gold-card member, Mr S., who was travelling with his elderly mother to Las Vegas (LAS) in First. My least favourite part of the SCCM job was the obligatory 'Senior's personal introduction to all First Class customers.' It felt forced and unnecessary, as these people probably often flew more frequently than us, and were well aware of how the game worked. The problem came when I had to chat to him and his mother in seats 4A and 5A. "Well, Simon...I'm not impressed with the service...". ("What service?" I thought to myself – "We've only been up in the air ten minutes...").

"Tell me more Mr S, and maybe I can do something about it…".

"Well, for a start, on boarding, no one escorted me to my seat, but that's okay as I could see you were busy." (Strictly speaking, it was crew no.'s 9, 10 and 11 whose responsibility this was). "Once I found my seat, my jacket wasn't hung up for me immediately, and it took several minutes for our drinks to come."

"I'm sorry to hear this: Is there anything I can do to redress this for you?" (The technique here is to give the customer the 'power' to suggest resolution.)

"No, not really, Simon – I just fancied a moan really!" (I looked at him, thinking "I have a full jumbo jet here with 300 people on board, plus staff-passengers using a handful of spare jump seats, and this guy is using up valuable time that I need to spend on running a smooth flight for the other 299, plus my crew and the flight crew!")

"I'm a Gold-card member Simon, and I've been travelling BA for 24 years."

"I know, I've read the paperwork."

"Do you know how much my fully flexible fare in First to Las Vegas is, Simon?"

"Yes, Mr S, I'm well aware." (He told me anyway, emphasising the figure for good measure…).

"Eleven thousand pounds." (So, between him and his mum… double that.)

He then started a new tack, recognising the new fleet that we belonged to within the company. Regardless of the fact that I wasn't exactly pro-mixed fleet, I wasn't going to engage him in this, as he expounded on what he thought about the set-up.

"I have a CSD mate who told me…" (When he mentioned CSD, which stands for Cabin Service Director – the equivalent rank to me on the 'Legacy Fleet', I thought, "This guy knows too much, and he's been primed…"). I wasn't going to play ball with him, so I took a deep breath and prepared for my P45 on return to base a couple of days later….

"Well, Mr S, you'll know exactly why this fleet was set up then, won't you? Yes, cost-cutting under the guise of increased service. You'll also know that we only get two days' premium service training. You will know about our route system too and the open conflict between fleets." (I held my name badge out prominently.) "I tell you what, take my name and feed back on our conversation…they don't listen to us…."

He paused, before delivering his more considered reply: "Actually, Simon, they don't listen to us either!"

We agreed to disagree but as I left him to enjoy his cabin and the heightened inflight service, he dropped this one into the mix: "Simon, I notice you've got a Scouser (Liverpudlian) working in First. *What's a Scouser doing serving in First?!*"

I really had to hold my tongue to stop myself from saying something I later regretted, and opted for silence. Some people will stay the same and always have to be right. I left the scene politely, and discreetly told my trio in First to "do everything by the book as they're watching us like hawks".

Please don't tell us how to do our jobs!

Arguably my favourite response to suggestions of how we should do our jobs, was from a captain on an ORY (Paris-Orly) flight waiting to depart from LHR. It was a moderately busy A319 on a late afternoon in the week, and we were suffering a delay of about an hour, awaiting an ATC slot: nothing new and absolutely routine with Paris flights. I recalled this from my dispatch days at Bristol. Two Club Europe pax, one of whom claimed to be flight crew for Cathay Pacific, strongly urged me to talk to the captain about negotiating this or that, to get our slot put forward. We were in a state of readiness anyway for departure and knowing that at any moment our new slot could be given, I hesitated to venture in to see the boys in the flight deck, but had to be seen to be doing it, as I knew these pax were watching me. I discussed it with the captain who took off his headphones for a second, before erupting like Mount Etna: "It p****s me off when people try to interfere with us and try to tell us what to do! Why don't they just f*** off and leave us to do our jobs! How would they like it if we came into their offices and started telling them what to do?!!" You know something – as I smiled at him, nodding my head, I half-hoped that the sound had carried to seats 3D and 3F... As it happened, we were off-stand within about ten minutes. Leave us to it – that's why we are there. And yes, even captains swear from time to time.

Silver and Gold

At LGW, I was soon to get used to 'The Executive Club' with its three-tier (Blue/Silver/Gold) system of snobbery, and a fourth unseen level, (the Premier card), which was for those individuals who brought in at least £1m worth of continuous annual business to the airline. The line that used to grate on me the most was: "I'm a Gold card holder!" It was used so frequently that it almost became meaningless in its delivery, as if the world should suddenly stop and a fault line miraculously seal, defying nature, healing rifts and ultimately causing everything to be as it should be. The reality is, of course, that it was a coloured piece of plastic attached ostentatiously to a briefcase or a wheelie-bag handle with the same 'notice me' appeal of a crew tag.

To those of you reading this who are feeling incensed that I should look down with disdain on you who have spent so much on flying with the brand, then please wait until my punchline: Is it not the *airline* which has appealed to your sense of reward for loyalty, promising you this or that, and feeding you the line: "We value your custom and your business"? Just like Sainsbury's Nectar Card. We all want recognition, validation and reward, but maybe just maybe, the airline fed you a little bait like: "*Fly an extra four return journeys with us this year and we will give you two thousand air-miles and a one way Club-class journey free.*" You see, we have all been suckered by these everyday systems! Reward has its price in this world. (It reminded me of '*Titanic*' and the way the senior officer threw the dollar bills back at Cal when he tried to buy his way off the ship onto a lifeboat – the money couldn't save him.)

Still on this topic, despite all I have just written, we actually *did* recognise brand loyalty and on board we had to look after the 'Golds and Silvers' which was difficult on a short hop of 45 minutes. I don't have a big problem with the reward-scheme, but the self-importance that would often manifest itself should there be a delayed flight, an issue with seating or a pre-ordered meal not on board. One day, a seafood meal (SFML) was not onboard. When I broke the news up in the air apologising, the sole C-class traveller groaned, so I offered him champagne, if necessary four quarter bottles to take off as compensation. His response was: "You're not actually giving me anything I can't have already, are you? I'll take eight bottles." (Nice try.) I retorted with my final offer: "I can give you four as I have a busy flight coming back and it's all I can spare." He took the bag ungratefully and muttered something unintelligible under his breath. At £4/ bottle retail, compared to the £2 absolute maximum cost to produce the seafood meal, I would say he was probably ahead of the game, if a little hungry.

It took me several weeks to work out why a simple meal ordered for a premium pax wouldn't arrive on the plane in time; business travellers pay more for their seats for ticket flexibility and last minute changes to travel, so if a meeting finishes early or they have to stay on until the following day, they can usually change their flights without penalty as it's a ticket condition, hence the increased price in the first place. There is however no guarantee that a special meal will follow with the same speed as the change, and that explains why – with the best will in the world – it is sometimes not possible to get the catering to follow the booking.

Another thing I was to learn is the rule: "You never delay a flight for catering". Fog-bound in freezing Cork, Ireland, on a stretched ATR 72 at 07:00, we had an ATC slot which the captain (ex-Cathay Pacific jumbos) was patiently, yet nervously awaiting. Aware of this and my own predicament – how to pacify about 50 punters who weren't going to get anything to eat on the hour-long 'breakfast flight'. Despite frequent calls by radio, the catering truck was to miss our 'off-blocks' time by a couple of minutes as we rolled off the apron, onto the taxiway and into the clearing Irish mist….The handful of C-class passengers were the most vocal, telling me it was "the worst flight (they) had ever been on". What they didn't realise was that if I had stayed to greet the catering truck, overriding the captain, in favour of an easy-ride home without conflict from the cabin occupants, the aircraft would have been further delayed by having missed its slot, costing thousands of pounds. I would have received a personal reprimand from both Ops and my crew base-manager and many would have missed their connections at LGW. There we go, the bigger picture. I hope the fat-injected bacon and eggs in their small foil container, were worth the hassle.

Have a drink...

Heavy drinkers can come in many forms, from the secret drinkers like the eastern European ship crews who smuggled 500ml vodka bottles onboard in paper bags to guzzle during a breakfast service to the guy who cannot cope without several whisky miniatures during an hour-long flight. There are of course, those who take advantage...

I once operated a flight to LAS on the 777, where not only Club World was full, but every seat onboard too. A couple of months later they decided that the route was worthy of extra capacity, so switched it to the 747, adding a First cabin which increased the revenue dramatically. A full First on such a route could bring in maybe £150,000 alone, so it was worth it. Five male companions – three Norwegians, an Italian and a Greek gentleman – were travelling together in C-class, and began knocking back the welcome-Champagne before we had even closed the doors. They started to go for it up in the air, with a mix of red wine, beers, brandies and more champagne, getting louder and merrier, but not yet troublesome. The main man was well-built and assertive and at every opportunity ordered more for his throng. I had spoken to my crew and they were looking to me for what we should do, because it was going to get out of hand. This type of situation has to be delicately yet firmly handled, as although Club-pax are entitled to an abundance of free-drinks in proper glasses served on trays, there is no way they should threaten the peace of the cabin.

It was by now about two hours or so into the flight, and the meal service in Club was heading for the dessert/coffee round. 'Big-chap' came up to me and stated loudly that he wanted more drinks brought to his party. I told him the trolleys were out for the service and I couldn't do it just then, so I said I would do him 'a deal': wait 15 minutes, have some coffee in the meantime, and then I would come see them. He didn't like this answer, and tried to barge past the double trolley in the other aisle, to no avail. At this point I observed his face was reddening, reflecting a change in mood. Giving up, and thwarted by a pair of fifty kilo double-trolleys blocking both aisles, he went back to his seat, and this bought me 15 minutes to play with. Having stowed the trolleys, cleared in and earmarked what I would like to eat, I ventured down to the second Club cabin not knowing quite what to expect but hoping for the best. My judgement call had been right. Full of alcohol and of no use to anyone, the five grown men were fast asleep and didn't wake up until the plane touched down at LAS, seven-and-a-half hours later. Relief. A mix of bubbly, Argentinian Syrah, Stella and various spirits had rendered them useless, and they were still rubbing the sleep from their eyes on exit at D2L.

Alcohol wasn't the only problem you had to face. I heard a troubling retelling of an event by a fellow senior of an Airbus waiting to depart to somewhere like Budapest. A man sitting in 'Traveller class' and minding his own business was, without warning, punched in the face by a complete stranger sitting in front of him. It turned out that assailant had mental health issues, but that's still distressing for the victim. The blood was cleared up and the flight departed minus one – and rightfully so.

I let these next two 'customers' think what they liked, and to be honest, they could take their preconceptions with them. I was taking a food order in Club World on a US-bound flight, when two Israeli businessmen in their 50s started to talk indiscreetly in front of me, dropping suggestions that I was only there because I liked men in *that* way, and probably fancied *them* too. I kept a cool head, calm and professional. It would have been too easy to tell them that I was married with children. Far more effective would have been to recommend the pork steaks, and watch them stew. Good job I'm not like that.

Terry

Talking of children, in the days before my own kids, being a big kid myself, I would take delight in looking after UNMINS (Unaccompanied minors) on board. They would usually sit quietly, reading, drawing or playing a Nintendo. One nine year old lad called Terry, asked if he could visit the pilots as it was his first time on a plane. Terry wore glasses and reminded me of Stuart Little's brother: quiet, smart and surprisingly confident. Watch the quiet ones. I took him into the cramped ATR 72 flight-deck to see Nick and John, who welcomed him in and showed him how our flight to BRE (Bremen) was progressing. Terry asked lots of questions as

Nick pointed out the fuel gauges and radar headings and, as they spoke, Terry – who had obviously been doing some rapid mental calculations of his own – worked out precisely how much fuel burn they should be more efficiently working to, in order to save money. At this point, Nick thought it wise to announce: "Well Terry, thanks for coming along. Simon, I think it's time to show Terry back to his seat, as we're starting to get busier now. Bye Terry!" (Adopt NYC accent in the style of Goodfellas.) The truth was that the kid knew too much. One day he's gonna get whacked. Actually, you sensed that kids like Terry would probably become huge success stories, possibly ending up being accountants to people like Sting. (Ahem. Do you recall what happened there...?)

Other children were obviously being shuttled between divorced parents, often leaving the UK to visit their dads who worked abroad. There was a kind of sadness about this everyday fact of life for many children, caught in the middle of separation and being sent to and fro on their own for school holidays, thousands of miles away. My job was to get them settled, check on them periodically through the flight for loo trips and drinks, and otherwise leave them to it, so as not to be overbearing unless the flight was quiet and that way you could entertain them with your animal masks. Yes, every crew member should have one, and my favourite was the cow, followed by the rabbit as a close second. I kept them from my Bristol Airport days.

During my career, I have had to calm nervous ladies, help fill in landing-cards, organise groups of school kids and assist multitudes of people with all manner of disabilities. Unbelievably, I've never had to clean up sick, but I have had to fumigate toilets. Every now and then, you encounter someone you get the chance to talk to, usually in the galley. En route one day to BUD (Budapest), I got talking to an ex-USAF F-15 Eagle pilot, who was now a fully trained Presbyterian minister/chaplain. He looked very much like a pilot, in his brown leather flying jacket covered in military patches, and told me about the time he had "ejected at about Mach One after a double engine flame-out at 15,000ft". His body was supported by metal, and he didn't know how he survived. He came to the only obvious conclusion that God still wanted him to complete a mission for Him. And wear a leather flying jacket.

On another couple of routine European flights, I encountered a chap who said he recognised me from previous flights, and what stunned him was my use of his name, and how I remembered it from boarding. Don't ask me how, but I tried a little experiment every flight to see if I could remember the odd surname and found it would surprise people greatly on leaving the plane, that somehow they were important enough to be addressed personally. It was something we were told to do only with First, but I figured why not others? Sometimes I would chat to famous musicians, actors, businesspeople, politicians and heads of state. They were all just travelling somewhere else and it broke up the routine for all of us.

Travelling to Kiev, Ukraine one morning, we had among the guest-list a junior football team and parents, so the group numbered about 40, among the 120 or so pax on the A320. Their Kosher meals (KSML's) were loaded onto the aircraft frozen, and the pax traditionally have to break the seals themselves to comply with their Jewish religious traditions. The problem was that we couldn't get the ovens to heat up the hot entrees, despite using forward galley capacity too, with only a couple of pax in Club. I kept the pax updated by PA, and we amended the service so it was just a little bit scrappy compared to what it should have been, but they were without their hot breakfasts on a three hour flight. The captain joined me at the doors on disembarkation and he noted how happy the pax were, despite their lack of food. How you handle and communicate with people on your flights can really turn a situation around, and that was extremely mild compared to many of the mishaps I have endured. On the return flight I carried a well known UK garage star/ DJ who slept through the entire journey in One-Foxtrot. I got a way more interesting conversation out of his tour manager who usually sound-engineered for a well-known pastiche rock band with an appropriately-titled debut album years earlier: 'Permission to Land'. (Those guys had come to see my band play in London years earlier.)

Dreaded flights

So, what are the flights that we dread? Anyone who has endured the 'joys' of a 'night Tel Aviv' (TLV), will know that these are traditionally the most demanding and soul-destroying flights for a C/A. It is known that Israeli pax can come across as rude and demanding, which is hard for us Brits to comprehend, but that's just the way it is. Once you get to know them, they soften. A night-flight to Magaluf or Tenerife is going to bring out the boy-racers and the divas in force, and you are going to be cleaned out of lager and vodka. There will be raised voices, singing and disturbance. I've even heard of some girls (pax) on those flights wearing no-knickers. (Not guilty: I swear by M&S, sometimes even Primark too, plus I'm not a girl.) You have to employ the skills of assertiveness and diplomacy on such flights. A full Dublin with a pay-bar could see you rushed off your feet just on a drinks-round, leaving you with the marvel of empty trollies.

Any delayed flight – charter or scheduled, will bring out the worst in pax. Imagine a four-hour delay, where on top of the normal wait, which can be excruciating enough, the extra hours with your children crying and being demanding can quite easily send you over the edge, especially if you're abroad and no one official seems to be communicating with you. Add to this, it is usually a three-hour delay or over that triggers refreshment vouchers, and what if you have run out of milk and nappies? This is all too common a scenario unfortunately. By the time you get on board you're probably at the end of your tether, but sometimes all it takes is a smiling face, and the relief on the faces of the pax is all too clear: "We're finally going home…." The sight of the cabin and a comfortable seat, the familiar boarding music playing through the speakers, and a smiling face can do wonders.

If, in some small way, our actions can grant you sanctuary and the absence of stress, then this is why we are here. Pretty soon, "the lights will be dimmed and if you wish, you may fall asleep for the duration of the flight, but just make sure your seatbelt is fastened and visible in case of turbulence". How many flights I have operated where this is the case. It's almost like a rescue mission just to bring stranded holidaymakers back from what had been a perfect break. In common with so many flights, it doesn't take long for the dull vibration and smooth-travel through the skies to lull you into sleep – even in a fairly uncomfortable seat with a 32" pitch.

So, this was a brief excursion into the world of pax. Now, I'm going to take you into the world of crew members and what we are really like. Brace, brace!!

Chapter Seven

Aircrew psychology

Somewhere in all of this, I felt a little lost. Call it an identity crisis, but I was not a woman and I was not gay – at least, not to my knowledge – so I was stuck in a no-man's land, where people wondered what to call a guy who is an air-hostess. Was I Ken to Barbie? Would you call me an air-hostess? Would you call me Glenda? I actually answer to most things, so feel free. I felt a little like Peter Parker, where his struggle is "Who am I?", and still often feel the same way. How do you define a man in this context? Even the pilots used to look at me slightly sympathetically as if to say, "Poor thing – you really wanted to be a pilot all along, and you fell into this!" I was once even propositioned by a man as we taxied onto stand at LGW. As we were making polite conversation, he asked me: "So, do you fancy meeting up tonight?" I shuddered inside, and instead of telling him that I wasn't gay and to get lost, I simply looked out of the window in shock and mouthed, "Sorry, I've got an early rise tomorrow." (This was so ineffective a reply that I might as well have said, "Sorry, love, I'm washing my hair…"). Unfortunately, I made the mistake of telling Brendan, the captain (the one from the missing nose wheel at RTM), as we were awaiting the crew bus. I can't print his reply, but he and the F/O were in stitches, while I needed a cup of weak tea to calm me down. (These were the same two pilots on the missing nose wheel incident, and it was my turn to go white....)

What sort of person would do this job?

In this next part, I want to look at the personality types I encountered while working in this profession. It would be too easy to compartmentalise people and to disregard the fact that we are all complex. However, it would be accurate to say that the sort of person who would do well as a cabin attendant would be an extrovert, easy to get along with, naturally smiley, a good listener, a clear communicator, and – perhaps above all – a perfect fit in a team. Believe me, if you're stuck in a confined space all day, you want to work with a team you can actually get along with, so colleagues need to be carefully chosen.

People came from an astonishing array of backgrounds, countries and cultures, leaving their pasts behind to become air cabin crew. Along the way, I met boys and girls who were ex-firefighters, ex-military personnel and a surprising number of former police officers, a handful of whom had been very high up in the Met. Gordon ran his family's business as an undertaker. Nadia was a former trapeze artist. Baldy B had worked in the Passport Service. Single-mums, driving-instructors, plenty of graduates, pilots-in-training, businesspeople, teachers, catering workers, retail employees, personal trainers, construction workers, recruitment consultants, holiday reps, nurses, dancers and many other professionals had made the break from their respective fields to try out something they had always wanted to do, but it had not been the right time before. What was the attraction? Glamour? Danger? The uniform? Travel perks? Hotels and suitcases? Shampoo containers and instant coffee sachets? I was quite easy to please, as all of the above ticked my boxes, including the obvious: working on an airliner isn't exactly an everyday sort of role. It is always going to be at least mildly interesting, if not downright unpredictable. The training prepares you for eventualities that you might never see personally in a quarter of a century.

Often the hardest decisions I faced, were how to smuggle two more iced doughnuts out of the breakfast-room for later, or how to pack all this chocolate to get it back to England. The free hotel soaps, conditioners and coffee were a secondary concern- you could always find some space in the hold bag. The larger items were a pain, like the bodyboard I carried back from DEN, and the Stanley tool box I took through PHX for one of my sons. I could feel the pax stares at the departure gates, reminding of the words in The Cult's 'She Sells Sanctuary', especially with the bodyboard as it was January and freezing outside when I carried it through. Call me blasé, but the actual procedures of operating a flight are so regimented that it is incredibly safe. That means there's usually time enough to actually enjoy the work, and get on with the business of giving pax 'a pleasant flight' as the saying goes.

What exactly are the airlines after, when they recruit for these air-crew roles? I can now tell you, after enduring a ground role and four flying roles, that I am none the wiser. Sure, they can dress up the post-interview analysis, the elaborate scoring matrix, and amateur-psychologist techniques, but how some people slipped through the net, I will never know. There were things that recruiters should have picked up on with some candidates I worked with, like a latent aggressive nature, lone wolf tendency, moodiness, a manipulative character or an inability to put others first. That said, the vast majority of colleagues were a pleasure to work with, and get through a double-duty with, a long night-flight or a there-and-back so busy, it was over before you knew it. If you, dear reader, work in an office with a team you see daily and know fairly well, this next bit will be hard to fully appreciate, but it's owing to the training that it works.

Crew members don't work on a formal shift pattern with earlier and lates, nor do they work within a regular group of colleagues assigned to each flight. They are loners, who arrive as freshmen to each duty, knowing only the names of their co-workers in advance on the next month's rosters, which come out a week or two before the end of each month. In a small airline of maybe 50 cabin crew for example, it would be normal to know everyone and to work with people you know regularly over the course of a few weeks. However for a large international airline such as BA there were between the three fleets at LHR, a total of around 14,000 cabin crew alone. When I joined early in 2011, my fleet had only just been set up and was being broken in, like a new pair of leather boots. Then, there were about 200 fellow crew-members, but by the time I had left 18 months later, there were 10 times as many colleagues on that fleet alone, owing to aggressive expansion by the company. Therefore, personnel must fit into the team-ethos seamlessly, as soon as they arrive at work.

Airlines aren't great payers, so people would moonlight to bring in extra cash. I knew several part-time models and wedding-singers. Plenty of crew ran their own businesses too, such as cafes, fruit & veg shops and florists. Others were into PR and events management, others traded in retro clothing, while I bought and sold vintage drums from time to time, which I still do. One quiet guy got caught out because his phone-booth advert, displayed at various locations in Brighton, showed him in his BA uniform. I can only imagine the parting conversation in the manager's office, "bringing an airline into disrepute". I don't think we ever saw him on board again. Watch the quiet ones. Another lady was a dancer in a club, which she was quite open about and, to be honest, when you looked at her, you could quite easily imagine it. Apparently she had danced with Bob Geldof, but kept him at a distance as he was quite hairy by all accounts.

Numbnuts

There is usually one character who stands out, and simply because he (and it's usually a 'he') is so outrageous, quick-witted and risqué, yet so likeable, he can be forgiven a lot. That person used to call me 'Numbnuts' in his soft Scottish accent. The first time I met him, three of us were about to embark on a busy 45 minute hop to AMS on the ATR 72. Between flights, while we waited in the sun next to the plane we had just used, I chucked him a can of Diet Coke from the bar trolley which he chastised me for, asking me if I was calling him fat. He got me back badly during the pre-flight safety-demo 30 minutes later: I was pointing out the window exits at the front of the plane, and just at the moment when he turned around from the C-class curtain at the rear of the ATR to point out his nearest exits, he pulled a goofy suntanned-face down the cabin behind everyone's backs. I struggled to compose myself, in front of the pax who were wondering why tears were rolling down my face, but it got worse in flight. During the drinks round he asked me, "Simon-doll, could you pass me two whiskies, please pet?" As I held the miniatures out, he gently stroked my hand in full view of the pax. He told me later that at that moment I went white.

This was to be the start of a beautiful platonic relationship confined to bumping into each other in the crew room, between a full-on lifetime camp C/A who lived in Brighton and a reluctant air steward who being straight and a little sensitive at times often felt like a fish out of water in the industry. He would do all he could to try to persuade me to leave my straight path and join him for unbridled pleasures, but I was – and am not – programmed that way. I am a red-blooded man with Venetian roots.

He certainly had the stories. Indian flights, call bell going for a while, and he re-enacts going up to the illuminated seat: "Yes Mr Patel. What would you like?" Response: "I have been fingering you for a long time but still you are not coming!" Answer, quick as a flash: "Well doll, you've obviously been using the wrong finger!" Same flight: "Wanting Walking-Johnny, Walking-Johnny!" The reply: "Well pet, you may be wanting but you're not getting!" It was as if the whisky had walked.

Another one: fed up of being constantly embroiled in arguments with C-class pax, he tells how he would sometimes finish a conversation: "Here's 10p doll – go and phone someone who'll listen!" He would sometimes announce his crew names: "… and working at the back of the aircraft we have Minjita…". We had no-one by that name.

He would look at me sometimes in passing and, I don't know why I am smiling as I write this, but he would implore me: "Come take me way from all of this Numb-nuts, and make an honest woman of me…". He and I operated only a handful of flights together and a bit like the two kids in the classroom who have to be split up, because all they do is giggle when they sit next to each other, well, that was Numb-nuts and I. I ended up calling *him* Numb-nuts in the end.

We once operated a there-and-back to RTM, the outbound (O/B) being pretty quiet. He found enough time to pester me relentlessly, starting with the following question: "What colour underwear are you wearing, doll?" "Red", I answered skilfully, as it was indeed the truth. "Show me!" he barked. "I ain't showing you!" I retorted, but Numb-nuts was hard to turn down, and his insistence led me to pull my trousers down in the ATR's cramped rear galley, displaying my then-new M&S tight red trunks (which I must say were very comfortable and of supremely good quality, as you might expect from M&S.) "There – happy?!" I asked, to which all he could do, was look me up and down with a nod of approval and a slight purr. My trousers were securely re-fastened and the flight continued uneventfully. If he was in a charitable mood, he would extend the invitation to join him: "Come to Brighton this evening, doll – you can play bingo with me and all my homosexual friends!" I never did.

Juniors

Junior new entrants: wide-eyed and eager to please, full of fresh motivation, they find everything interesting, and nothing is too much trouble. It doesn't normally take longer than three or four months for the sheen to wear off, and the realisation that this is most definitely the honeymoon period to kick in. Girls (and boys) on airport standbys sit down on sofas in crew rooms to chat and moan, dissect and pick, as they come up for air from their phones, or *Hello!* magazine. They are joined by more willing colleagues and, bit by bit, in quite a subtle fashion, the initial flame of enthusiasm is replaced by a gritty realism. Some of these girls can be easy-pickings for randy pilots, who seduce them with their obvious charms and rings on their sleeves, a time-honoured and predictable dance.

There was a phrase often used by new entrants as they gained experience: "This isn't a job – it's a lifestyle." I disagreed – it's just a job. The funny thing is, I used to come across colleagues who appeared be in love with themselves. They were young, attractive, fun-loving, looked good in a uniform, were well-travelled and seemingly in control. That's easy when you're single, able to disguise emotions well, use a credit card like a magic wand and have a self-cultivated image. I remember one girl, travelling on the crew-bus, with whom I had worked only a couple of weeks before. I tried to catch her eye several times to say a quick "hello", but gave up, because the glazed-eyes 'celebrity look' she was giving off made it obvious she felt she was superior in some way. I hope she wasn't like that in the cabin, but having worked with her, I had the suspicion she was.

Another girl was so self-absorbed that she delighted in telling colleagues about her designer-shopping experience in the States, as apparently shoppers were able to tell she was 'crew.' Yet another, years earlier, had a conversation with me in the galley preening her ego verbally, because she had attained 'purser' status. (By the way, seniors can also be known as pursers, but this has relatively little to do with handling money. A purser can be the SCCM on a smaller aircraft usually, and be a section-senior on larger aeroplanes. I have come across the phrase *'chef de cabine'* on Air France, and *'cabin chief'*. 'No.1' used to be a pretty standard term, especially used by cleaners wanting the senior's signature on turnarounds.) I understood why this was so important to many: it's the age-old need for identity, and for a feeling of success. A role in the air can be unattainable to many – just see the statistics for those turned down at application. Apparently, around 30,000 applicants a month go for Emirates alone, probably the same 30,000 who go for many of the other airlines. Just to have made it in through the door says something about the person, I guess. My advice: don't act like a diva, it's mainly tea and coffee. They should have been a little more self-effacing, like Suzanne, the ex-Concorde SCCM who trained us: "I'm the chief sandwich-dispenser on the 767!" (If it's any help, remember that I made my dog cry when I landed my first airline job. Dogs are great for bringing you back down to earth.)

Comedians

Buoyant comics: granted, I fell into this category, simply because "You can't keep a good man down", as one of my friends used to say. (He also used to sing out loud after closing time, "A short life and a gay one", even though he was as straight as a bamboo cane.) No matter, up in the air you rely on humour, if only because it's so bizarre it's almost laughable at what is physically happening. We are being propelled at around 500 miles per hour, through clear skies at about 30,000ft above the earth, with an outside air temperature of minus 50 degrees Celsius.

One of the best stories I heard was from Andy at Air 2000, when seven of us were 'deadheading' (non-operating crew flying as pax) up to GLA (Glasgow) and then onto to AGP, to collect a plane-load of pax flying back from Spain to LGW. We were in the departure lounge at GLA, and he told us about a highly annoying retired couple on a TFS (Tenerife). Simply because they were 'Sovereign passengers' (i.e. they had paid about £20 each more for a couple of extras), they acted like royalty, and at every opportunity from boarding to being seated to being moved to their 'exclusive' cabin on the holiday flight, reminded Andy and all around that they were Sovereign passengers in haughty pompous tones. It got to the drinks round about 15 minutes into the flight, and the gentleman flashed his Sovereign vouchers accordingly with a louder than necessary reminder of their status. Andy asked them what they would like to drink. "Two gin and tonics. We shall use our Sovereign vouchers." Quick as a flash, Andy replied: "Would you like ice and lemon, you t***?!" The gentleman roared, "What did you say?!" The cool-as-a-cucumber air steward, taking advantage of the air-con system, simply responded, "I said, would you like ice and lemon with *that*?" Situation stabilised, and one-nil to the cabin attendant. What a Sovereign.

An evening turn-around in a snow-filled Zurich would allow me to get my own back on the F/O, who had made 'amusing' remarks about my lack of skills to the pax over the PA. (Here's a tip for you: don't believe *everything* you hear from the pilots when they address you in the cabin. (On another duty, I had supposedly landed the role of 'Joseph' in the West End and it was my last flight. I had an endless stream of congratulations from those disembarking and I remained professional throughout.) While he was carrying out the walk-around checks, I raced down the steps and rolled a snowball so large that I could barely carry it back into the cabin, and waited by Door 1R, judging the moment when he should be passing beneath me. He must have known something was afoot, as the door above him suddenly flew open and the 10kg compacted ice-ball came his way. With the instinct of a gazelle, he darted out of the way laughing, sliding in the snow below. I admit, it was me who then started a snowball fight inside the cabin, leading to some puzzled looks from boarding pax, at how much snow could actually enter a plane, compared with what was outside.

'Stephen' was my favourite Tristar captain, with whom I only managed to work with twice. What endeared me to him were his welcome PAs. He would come out of the flight deck pre-departure, and use the SCCM's PA handset by D1L to give his welcome in full view of the pax, or at least the first 150 or so, who were seated in the forward sections. "Good morning, ladies and gentlemen, this is your captain speaking. In case you can't see me, I'm the short, bald one standing at the front! Har, har, har…! It's going to be good weather down to Lanzarote today, and for those of you wanting to travel to Geneva, I'm sorry – you're on the wrong flight! Har, har, hargghh!" Priceless. I liked him immediately. On another occasion, my favourite Tristar captain announced en route to the Canaries, that it was "Ben Groom's 18th birthday, and we have a smashing member of the crew –Simon – who has volunteered to sing you 'Happy Birthday', Ben. Over to you, Simon!" I panicked, as I saw Tina and Dawn laughing from the mid-galley, while I was trapped in the cabin doing a drinks round. Was I going to sing to 400 people through the PA system? Not likely. Now, of course I would, being older, but not necessarily any wiser. I'm pretty good at harmonies, by the way….

The veteran

The seasoned veteran: every airline will have these in their ranks. A lady or gentleman who has been flying a long while will look visibly older as they carry the worn features of a battle-scarred life of flying. As I explained in Chapter Two, if an autopsy were carried out, their insides would most likely resemble a person double their age, as that's what long-term flying does to you. They are the sort of cabin crew whom the passenger might trust a little more to get things done, or to advise on how to deal with a missed connection, lost luggage, or how to pacify you in a panic attack. In terms of their treatment of pax, just like the other categories of crew, you can't generalise, and it will be pretty hit-and-miss as to whether they delight in serving others or not. A good one will have a glint in their eye, and be the sort of person who you could knock around with for a three-day trip, and not get bored. If you get a bitter one, they can ruin the flight with one stern expression and an attitude to match. Their ill-fitting jackets are often deliberately unbuttoned, their security passes swinging, and they will give off an air of superiority to pax and colleagues alike. They may smile from time to time, but don't be deceived, as they can turn into Rottweilers if they are challenged in any way. These people should have changed careers years earlier, but remain because either the money's too good, they are fearful of change or they can't see themselves doing anything else before retirement. There is a story my colleague/ trainer Chris told me, about boarding a flight at Seattle for LHR in the late Nineties, and, in his words: "Sat on a bar box, arms folded, with a jacket draped over his shoulders was a bitter queen, *smoking* and barely acknowledging the pax as we got on! He was muttering something like, 'Enjoy your flight', but it sounded so rude!" Maybe this queen should have found a different throne and some proper subjects....

SCCMs

Senior cabin crew: It took me a while to realise this, but if you are reading this as an outsider looking in, (which is exactly how I felt at times working *inside* the profession), then please take careful note next time you are on a plane journey, and watch the cabin crew members carefully. Usually, if you are boarding through the main door, you will be greeted by a slightly older crew member, who can be distinguished by a title on their name badge, a particular coloured-tie or scarf or, on some airlines, stripes on their jacket cuffs. (If you can't see him/her and the curtain is drawn in the galley, then they are probably sobbing after a relationship breakdown with their ex, and can't bear to face the general public. That, or they are pretending to get hot-towels ready while texting their partner.) These uniform emblems should indicate seniority, and this character, the SCCM or No.1, is third in the chain of command after the Captain and then the First Officer. The reason for me asking you to look at the crew members carefully, is that it is largely the SCCM who sets the mood for the flight, and this starts from the moment they enter through the briefing door an hour or two before the flight, while you are busy checking in, or heading to the departures lounge, where the stores pretend their prices are 20% less than the high street. If the crew are happy and eager, they could either be disguising their anxiety well, or hopefully, they have been validated by the Senior and empowered to do their jobs well with minimal interference. The Senior's impact will be felt by the whole cabin. Call it 'transference' if you will, but it is a lesson that I learned on many occasions, from being a junior all the way through to leading teams myself. His/her impact will travel faster than the aircraft itself, and the passenger should pick up on it pretty quickly. That's why I tried to 'do a deal' with my colleagues that they would support each other, not back-bite, nor try to tell me what to do, and in return I would treat them with respect and not lord it over them. It was an approach that on long-haul seemed to work especially well, where there is sadly much more to potentially go wrong.

The charter airlines in the UK had reputations to preserve, but one of the perhaps unwanted (but definitely-encouraged aspects), was 'the stern factor' in many of their seniors. I heard stories of harsh, authoritarian women in their 30s and 40s especially, who seemed to take their roles as being worthy of regal stature, demanding fear and subservience from those who worked beneath them. I endured a handful myself, and their fixations were well-known, so you knew you could prepare yourself psychologically if you saw their names on your roster. As a guy, I generally had very little hassle, but I felt for a lot of the young, pretty girls whose looks and willingness to please could be bait for the SCCM sharks that governed the waters on board. Check out this next illustration: maybe I was too young and too pretty....

Banjul, Gambia, East Africa, early 1997

My heart wasn't really in it, and I knew we were being stitched up, but Air 2000 were one of a handful of UK airlines, along with Airtours and Monarch, who had been given special dispensation by the CAA (Civil Aviation Authority) to operate Banjul flights, there and back in one day. It was deemed reasonable to make the 12-hour total return flying-time, plus check-in, turnaround and post-flight hours legally acceptable, equating to a total duty time of around 16 hours. (As the check-in time goes further into the daytime, post 09:00, the rough rule is that you can legally work for far longer.) You can understand why a Banjul wasn't especially attractive, apart from being an hours-building exercise, and worth an extra few pounds to put in your petrol tank. Even less attractive was the proposition of working under an SCCM with the reputation of being a dragon. Great, not even my smile was going to save the long day....We completed the briefing (during which it became obvious that this was not going to be an easy day, as the air was full of tension, with the way she looked at us, and how she quizzed us), then the seven of us joined the two ex-RAF pilots downstairs at security. Once through, as usual, we took the crew-bus out to meet the long thin 757, which was being loaded on one of the stands at North Terminal.

On board, once the safety checks had been completed, it was my job to look after the catering. We were return-trip catered, meaning that the inbound trolleys for the Banjul – LGW sector were loaded in the hold, and would be switched on the turnaround. First mistake: I didn't check it properly, and we were down a handful of meals, including several vegetarian (VGML) and 'special meals' (SPML). I was in a rush, because hawk-eyes (the SCCM), with her heavy charcoal eyeliner, was standing over me, flapping and commenting on the poor quality of the whole crew. When someone is in a position of responsibility and they act with little decorum or respect for others, the overall mood is deflated. You have to work harder as a team to keep afloat and compensate for a bad atmosphere. The rest of what happened was the routine blur: the girls put their black gloves on, checked their hair and lipstick, and took boarding positions, pax boarded via the jetty at D2L, sweets came around in baskets, the door was closed after 20 minutes and the full Boeing was ready – with minimal delay – to depart. Off we went, and the mood deteriorated up in the air.

I am sure that the headphone-wearing pax, completely absorbed by the IFE (in-flight entertainment) had not a clue that the senior was spending every 15 minutes or so walking from front to rear, it transpired to decimate the characters of those who were under her in one galley, then back to do the same in the other galley. The problem was, looking back, that she had probably been allowed to do this over a long period of time – maybe a couple of years, so you can imagine how many had been infected by her disease. Not only that but way more importantly, she had so damaged the crew rapport, that if anything had happened (a mid-air emergency for example), the stability of the crew as a whole would have been affected by her personality and the team-cohesion rocked. I hope I am not being melodramatic, but it only takes one bad apple to ruin a barrel. I can remember one of my female colleagues whom I had recently trained with – a former chef – coming up to me in the aisle while I was serving coffee on the outbound flight. She must have seen my face, with some of the shine knocked off it by the barrage of abuse from the SCCM, and simply came up to me and gave me a light kiss on the cheek in front of everyone. She will never know how her act of tenderness helped me to keep going.

The turnaround came as a merciful reprieve, and the trolleys were exchanged. The aircraft was a hive of activity with cleaners inside, so I popped down the steps and onto African tarmac to get a taste of some real air, warm and soothing. The Monarch and Airtours 757s landed shortly after ours, and so it was that the Brits invaded The Gambia, with their eagerly-awaited spending power to keep the tourist economy going. Talking of economy, I caught sight of some truly African entrepreneurship in the B-hold, where obviously the chief baggage-handler had taken it on himself to sell some of our pax *Daily Mails* to his colleagues, who were lining up around the cargo door. I smiled at the goings-on, as it was welcome relief to be out of the tube that had been infused with an awkward and unnecessary atmosphere for the last several hours.

Off again after the one hour turnaround, and the powerful Rolls-Royce RB211 high bypass turbofans propelled us once again into the evening skies, leaving Banjul behind to head home – six hours away. I ventured into the flight deck from time to time with food and drinks, and remember the co-pilot Andy, in the right hand seat – a gracious guy, keen to point out the coastline we were following below as we followed our tracking on the Honeywell to the UK. The autopilot, as usual, kicks in not long after the initial climb, leaving the pilots to monitor the radios as well as the flight systems, engine/fuel performance and weather en route. I unwillingly left the sanctuary and quiet reprieve of the flight deck, and went back into the cabin, feeling the tension straightaway.

The catering mistake had given the Senior more ammunition against me, as we now had to offer food from our crew-supplies to the couple of vegetarian pax who were without their meals. This wasn't ideal, but it's an acceptable practice, and is used from time to time to make sure a fare-paying customer actually eats. This of course didn't stop the Senior from reprimanding me for my stupidity. I accepted the blame and carried on with the duty-free sales (which is where we earned our commission of about 2%) : another 20 to 30 minutes out in the cabin, selling cartons of cancer sticks and useless fluffy toys. Unfortunately, I gave the No.2 at the back (second-in-charge) a bit of a headache to work out a double entry/refund issue on the in-flight sales computer, and the last thing I needed was another senior crew member on my back. It was to be rectified back at base.

The last job on disembarkation was to collect charity money in envelopes from departing pax, and there's a reason I mention this. You're probably waiting for some sort of punchline to this flight: there isn't one, apart from saying that the six hours back, being a quasi-night flight, landed about midnight and back in the crew-room, we counted the takings. 'Hawk-eyes' now looked tired and unkempt, her red jacket unbuttoned and was wearing a glazed and slightly bored look. I drew a line underneath this flight and biked home exhausted. It was to be many months later that I discovered something about 'Hawk-eyes', which my then-girlfriend told me. She had been dismissed from the company, not as I expected for an awful attitude and poor leadership, but something way more down-to-earth. She had finally been caught stealing charity money. Poetic justice indeed. The moral of the story? Airlines: you should invest time in making sure that your SCCM's are encouragers, people-focussed, motivated and insightful. Pay them well, train them better in CRM (Crew Resource Management) and the rewards will be reflected in your increased customer satisfaction results, reputations and even payloads.

The reality of the job

Whilst working at LHR more recently, I kept myself to myself, as my life was back home, and this was just work. What became quickly apparent is that all was not as it seemed with this new set-up, and the initial euphoria that many junior colleagues experienced on being chosen, was rapidly tempered by the realisation that they were being micro-managed, and heavily-penalised financially, to keep them on their toes. Although they loved the job itself, most were unable to make ends meet. Being able to afford normal life, alongside job satisfaction, is the main reason you go to work. I was trained in 'end-to-end people management', which I asked my training-manager about, and he replied, "Yes, Simon – it's about hiring and firing." The fleet was an accountant's dream: pay new joiners peanuts, squeeze the best out of them, increase the customer satisfaction levels to the roof, and put the company back into profit levels it used to enjoy. And internationally, many airlines were already using this template. Well into my career, I asked my then immediate manager –Andy– what the deal actually was: "Andy, be frank with me. How long are people actually expected to be here? One to two years?" His reply: "Uh… two to three years and then we move them on…". (Just as I thought, and the shame was that the majority of my colleagues took it all on face value and were hoping for longer careers than this, while some had a plan that might fit in neatly with that of their employer: to treat the job as a short-term stop-gap until they found out what they really wanted to do….)

The day-to-day experience (which I found out was taken from the Harvard business model), meant constant service improvements to the point of obsessive detail, reminders of standards and penalties, and a seeming lack of humanity. Wear them out then allow them to expire, as there were queues of replacements on a continuous recruitment cycle. There was seemingly an allowable leaving rate of about 25%. I scoured my contract for a tiny loophole, but my legal training could not help me. It was watertight and, once signed, it was there in black and white. The lawyers had drafted an impenetrable document, so hats off to them. I even found out from a colleague in-the-know that this had been planned for many years, with all the secrecy of the CIA and had even been given a project name. I was amazed that more people didn't see through it. The airline probably had to do this belt-tightening exercise to continue, but it looked deliberately divisive.

The 'new fleet' was outwardly distinguishable in a couple of ways: girls wore Fifties-style hats sporting a tasteful chrome Speedwing, while a more subtle giveaway was the buttoned jackets at all times to sharpen up the slack uniform standards that had been allowed for so long. Crew members on old contracts were anxious about "the new fleet taking our jobs away." New joiners were worried about how they could survive, as all I saw and heard about was people telling me just how much they depended on their credit cards to exist month by month. Somewhere at Waterside HQ, senior management teams would be looking at spreadsheets on large screens, comparing reduced allowances expenditure, quicker turnarounds, higher scores on global surveys and the profit margins compared to existing set-ups. Profit and loss, SWOT analyses, NPVs and share capital were all under the microscope and the trolley-dolly brigade were only a couple of miles away from this world. This new set-up didn't please many on the other two main fleets and, without getting political....

Jaws takes the bait...

I heard a story from the same training-manager about a girl who had turned up for her first flight duty at the crew car park next to Runway 27 Left. After 15 minutes of desperate searching, she finally found a space in an upper storey and parked up, anxious to get to Crew Report Centre (CRC) in time. There was an older hostie nearby who, on seeing her hat-box, announced sternly, "You can't park here – it's for Worldwide." (BA's long-haul fleet.) The poor girl frantically searched for another space and almost missed her briefing, arriving at CRC in tears. That manager took her by the hand and went from room to room, in a effort to locate the woman who had lied about a car parking policy that never existed. Sadly they never did find her.

I was waiting for the bus from the car park at about 06:30 one summer morning and fell into conversation with a colleague in her late 40s, about the Quantas A380 we had just seen abort its landing far in the distance on the other runway parallel to 27 Left. She asked me where I was off to, and I said it was 'an office day.' The other two fleets had no such thing as 'office days': you were either at the airport for a flight, or off duty. Her face changed completely, and she started to tear into what the new fleet stood for, and how we were "responsible for dividing the airline, which used to be fantastic until this fleet came along…". The good old days of course. As I listened to her vacuous arguments and her one-sided reasoning, I could see she was missing one key detail: it wasn't the people who had joined this fleet that had "messed things up": it was her precious employer who, with deliberate strategic vision had had little choice but to set this up, as people wanted jobs and this airline was seen as the pinnacle to work for. She started to get personal, still jabbering on while we sat down at the back of the bus, so I waited to deliver my bait, which she seized with the animal instinct of the shark in *Jaws* going in for the gas bottle, seconds before the sheriff shot it into kingdom come: "Well, all the pilots seem to love flying with us…". I offered innocently, and waited a millisecond, before she exploded with raw emotion: "Well, they would do wouldn't they!!" and on it went. All I did was to light the blue touch paper. I could see that she was so obviously locked into a blinkered way of thinking, with no ability to see the bigger picture, and there were many more like her. If she were to fit into one of my previous categories it would be 'the seasoned veteran', Rottweiler edition. I'm pretty sure I bumped into her again as a staff pap flying home on one of my flights. She was very quiet. Watch the quiet ones.

Flight crew: the guys up front

Flight crew: love' em or loathe' em, they are the drivers, so I always treated mine with respect and took a test-the-water approach before unleashing my humour on them and an offer of cocktails. Every now and then you might work with a 'by-the-book captain', and you only needed to acknowledge the F/Os facial expressions to know what sort of day he was having. There were plenty of female pilots too – just not enough. Most captains were interesting characters: many had military backgrounds – probably mercenaries – and had stories you wouldn't believe. I asked Brian at Bristol what he used to fly in the RAF, as he was waiting to board a Dash 8 which I was dispatching. "Lightnings!" he replied quickly. I was amazed, as these interceptors were ahead of their time when they were introduced in the 1960s, with a vertical climb rate unmatched by anything built by man. "What were they like?!"

I enquired eagerly. His eyes lit up as he nodded with a smile, "Fast!" It's all he needed to say.

A couple of our captains at LGW fancied themselves as smooth and in control – much like their low-maintenance hairstyles – hence one of them earning the nickname 'James Bond'. The other would turn around from his seat to give me an exaggerated thumbs up with a serious Pierce Brosnan look, when I passed the cabin secure check in the RJ flight deck. I swear I'd seen that same look in 'GoldenEye'.

G had a prosthetic arm and was the nicest Antipodean gentleman. I often wondered how it worked. For some reason, his hand used to remind me of a character in Batman, and it wasn't Boy-Blunder. Someone matching his age and description ended up in the papers when a prosthetic arm became detached in the final approach phase, and the Dash was landed single-handed (no pun intended).

Paul, a youthful captain who could have been a model, called me into the flight deck one day asking me to have a look at a box with Chinese writing upon it, translated as 'dried scorpion'. As I opened it slowly, it started to scuttle violently, so I threw the whole thing up into the air, screaming bravely in front of both male pilots. (It turned out to be a piece of card powered by an elastic band.) Apparently it had been the best reaction yet, and had surpassed any of the girls' histrionics.

Captain Kev was 'a special friend' of Baldy B's, a youthful 747 pilot with a dirty laugh, like Sid James from the *'Carry On'* films. He told me a story about the time he was flying on an old airliner like a Viscount turboprop en route to Paris. He remembers dozing off and waking up the sleeping captain mid-flight. The yawning No.1 came into the flight deck, very slowly, incoherently announcing that she didn't know what was going on, but everyone was asleep in the cabin. Quickly, Kev realised he had forgotten to pressurise the cabin properly, which was normally done with a foot lever as a pre-take off check. He thought carefully before admitting his mistake to the captain, who replied calmly in Queen's English tones: "I think we'll keep this one to ourselves, Kevin…". On disembarkation, apparently everyone got off saying a similar thing: "That was the best flight I've ever been on…".

I once came in from a late evening flight and went to bed. I woke up in the morning to say "Hi" to the guy in the other bed across from mine, and a dishevelled unshaven face I didn't recognise looked up at me. It wasn't one of my room-mates, so I adjusted quickly to the presence of a stranger. "The party must have been good," I remarked, to which he replied: "Yeah, I was all over the place: Tequila, vodka, beer – it was a great night!" We shook hands and I introduced myself. He did the same: he was the Chief Airbus training captain for the youthful airline that flies in red/white with a bearded entrepreneur at the helm. Those guys – they party hard. I made the tea….

The room-party, Roma and a Concorde-captain

I used to work with some real characters, and my faves were the old-boy pilots who had plenty of colour to add if we ever had a beer or two on short night-stops (aka 'split-duties'). One of the best stories was from a captain called Ian, who used to work for Royal Jordanian. With the passage of time, it became a little unclear as to whether or not this was the airline in question, but let's assume it was. He told us about an *apres-flight* room party in a hotel somewhere in the world in the Eighties. Plenty of drinks were flowing, in the good old days when you could happily raid the bar trolleys and, within reason, take pretty much what you liked from the plane, by all accounts. A pompous couple knocked at the door: he in a suit, she in a fur coat, both guests of the hotel and invited to the hedonistic shindig. As the door opened and they were invited in, the merriment and the noise of the whole crew partying, unsettled the woman, who obviously thought a good time was a five-course dinner in genteel company, with linen napkins. Apart from the hysterical laughter, she was especially outraged by the man behind Ian, on all fours with a trolley-dolly riding horsey on his back. "Well, I have a good mind to report this to the chief captain!" she announced, troubled at the spectacle of people having a good time, minus linen napkins, especially the equine couple. Her husband dutifully replied: "My dear – he *is* the chief captain!" Ian sniggered loudly as he recounted that one.

Another captain I enjoyed talking to was Pete, a short man with a knowing smile, a 1960s/70s veteran of BEA/British Eagle Days, then Air Zimbabwe. He used to take pleasure in pointing out a Monarch DC-10 at LGW which he used to fly in Africa. He would take me back to la *vita bella* of Italy, and speak of the happiest days he had with his girlfriend, living together in a caravan on the outskirts of Rome in the the 1960s. He could conjure up the sun, the cool wind and the simplicity with just a few words which recreated the image of actually being there in the Italian capital in the heady days of sixties liberation, Dean Martin and *Fiat Cinquecentos*. Even the idea of simply hanging out the washing next to the caravan, with the coffee brewing in the mocha, the rolling hills of Lazio peppered with cypress and pine trees in the distance, was deeply romantic.

I knew another particularly amiable captain – John – and it was impossible not to like him. He was always smiling, he was never far from a politically-incorrect comment and, having been an ex-Concorde captain as well as an RAF instructor, he was entitled to do *The Times* crossword on final approaches, steering with his knees to finish 32 Across. (As if you've never done it in your own car…tut tut….) My first flight with him was an AMS night stop and, as we walked down the concourse slightly ahead of the girls, I made conversation. "Isn't this the place where the little boy plugged the dam?" It turned out it was a dyke, and he had plenty to say about that. He was apparently caught out during a quick turnaround at Newcastle (NCL) one day as this next story –

possibly untrue – became infamous. 'Pre-boards' was the term given to anyone with a disability who required a little more time or physical help to get on the plane, hence it was standard to board these pax ahead of the main throng so as to save time during the high-pressure boarding process. When he looked out of the window and saw a wheelchair approaching, he cheerily announced to the two cabin crew over the PA: "Prepare to repel 50 Geordie ******s!" Unfortunately for him, the pre-board had been left until last for some reason, and the '50 Geordie ******s' were already on the plane enjoying his unique welcome over the PA. I think he had a bit of trouble filling in 11-Down at that point.

You could be privy to some of the most interesting things while in the flight deck, ranging from the pilots in a 747 pointing out oddities on a night departure from LAS (Las Vegas), to a pair of A320 flyers laughing out loud during the cruise, at the Austrian ATC word 'Machular' (apparently describing a Mach number) and the Glaswegian captain remarking: "Aye, it sounds like a Scottish Dracula!" Yes, flight crew – they certainly are at the top of their game.

Sam ended up working for Monarch as an F/O, and told me a funny story of the refuelling episode at ASM (Asmara, Eritrea, Africa). He and the captain were chatting in the 757 F/D (flight deck), when all of a sudden they both jumped, as there was a knock on the side window. Who on earth could that be at 20 feet above the ground? Well, it turned out to be the refueller who had appeared, as if by magic, standing on a mobile baggage belt which he had used to give himself a lift up to the flight deck. Sam opened the window and handed over the company credit card to the refueller, who processed the payment with his card machine, returned the card and floated backwards with a wave. They wondered why he didn't just enter the flight deck the usual way, via the steps, but maybe he had spent years perfecting this trick, and it probably made his day go quicker.

We had just landed back at base on a flight from Vienna on another afternoon, and I opened my door at 1L to greet the arrivals agent who took the internal mail from me. "How are they?" he asked of me before the first of the pax had approached the door. "Miserable," I advised... He shook his head: "*Austrian* used to bring in an A321 with all the famous Austrians painted across the fuselage." "I know – I've got that model at home", I replied. "Well," he continued, "I told them they were missing someone on the side. They asked me "Who?" and I said, "Hitler!" You should have seen their faces!" There's humour and there's irony, but there's also tact. Our man was perhaps a bit tactless, but he did have a point. Maybe he could have done with a bit more training?

A captain's intuition in Crete
However much cabin attendants are trained – a few weeks initially and then periodic refreshers – captains undergo 100 times more in investment, to ensure that they are fit to occupy that left hand seat. There are plenty of female pilots, by the way, just not half as many

as men who dominate the profession. A captain will see things that others perhaps don't. His eyes of experience see things that others might not see. He has the left hand seat on the flight deck for a reason. He stands on the ship's bridge with ultimate authority for all on board. He has made it to take the place of highest rank and has to maintain total focus. When Rich and I flew to JFK, there was a hydraulics problem the flight crew needed to sort out in the supersonic airliner, so no flight deck visits; they needed no distractions – captain's orders. (That was the year before the Air France disaster at CDG, which tragically ended in a fireball. Concorde's days were numbered for both of the operating airlines following that terrible day.)

On a night flight to Heraklion, Crete, perhaps 22 years ago, we ended up departing LGW a few hours late, however the pax for the inbound flight to London had been sent back to hotels for the night as the airport was closed, and we had a little problem. But first two rounds of beers for the entire crew of 16 members, before retiring to bed at 4 am local time in Greece. Being one of the very few straight guys didn't mean I couldn't hold my own (perhaps wrong choice of phrase). I announced to everyone at breakfast the next day, "Hey everyone – I slept with Rob…." The reality was I did sleep alongside him in the last remaining room with a only a double bed. He retorted with his dry Northern wit: "I arranged all the cushions like a natural barrier – there was more division in that bed than at the Berlin Wall."

Back to the problem. We walked out to the far corner of the apron where 'Alpha-Papa', our ageing white Tristar with red 'go-faster' stripes was parked, against a background of green trees with the deep blue Aegean sea glistening behind her. Despite the August sunshine on a peaceful Sunday afternoon, the airliner cabin without ground power, was an eerie dark tube. The only noises were the odd creak inside, and the sound of fan blades whirring in the wind outside. The captain, F/O and flight engineer took me out with them as they needed to me to guard the vicinity of engine two from stray personnel while they performed engine runs. A vintage Tupolev 154 Russian airliner being the only other aircraft there, the two made a duo of elderly characters still in active service. The captain climbed up a ladder into the cave of the Rolls Royce RB211 engine and drew a picture of the problem: He described it to us as he clambered out: three bolts holding a metal plate inside the engine – one in place, one sheared-off and one completely missing. This diagram was faxed to Caledonian/BA engineers at LGW, and a local aircraft engineer fixed the problem. I tell this story to illustrate how it was his intuition and long experience as a military captain, along with his decision to consult his immediate colleagues, that led him to investigate. I often joke with colleagues: "You can't buy experience". But it's true, as long as you remember that we are always learning, so stay receptive to new ideas and don't assume you know everything, because there is always something around the corner waiting to trip you up. That much I have discovered, even just from the airline world.

I found my pilot colleagues to be respectful, intuitive, and personable in the main. As much as I marvelled at their abilities in the flight deck, I think many of them were probably just as much in awe of how we handled a cabin full of fare-paying pax. Imagine coming from the relative peace of the front end, monitoring the displays, gazing out of the windows on the majesty of creation, and out through a door into the hustle and bustle of the work we do to ensure people fly with us again and again. It's like two different worlds separated by a locked door. Their world gave me a welcome reprieve from mine, so I would often pop in time-allowing, to write reports, have a change of scenery or simply snooze for an hour on a night flight if the time was right. Pilots call it 'controlled rest'.

We all have lives outside an aircraft tube and don't permanently go back and forth from airliner to hotel. Very often, the last thing you want to see is another hotel in another country, with time to kill before being picked up again to return to the airport. We have lives – real lives – with family members we are longing to return to, people we don't see eye to eye with, banks we have to approach for overdrafts or loans and things that go wrong with our homes, cars and day-to-day stuff, just like anyone else. Lifestyle or job? Sorry to disappoint, but it is just a job, with a twist....

Chapter Eight

Empty airports

If you've ever had the experience of sitting in an airport, either in the main concourse or check-in areas, or in the post-security departures zones in the middle of the night when you should really be tucked up in your bed, then you'll be well-acquainted with that slightly surreal feeling of being alone, apart from the elderly cleaner pushing his floor-buffer or the security guard doing his rounds between fag-breaks. One major airport from Tokyo to Athens, or Toronto to Prague, could almost be any other from around the globe these days. Modern airport terminals look as though they were built from the same plans: full of well-known brand shops, huge glass sheets, immaculate high gloss flooring, elevators in either polished stainless steel or glass, and endless corridors peppered with anonymous locked doors marked 'Staff only'.

Airports at these times are like ghost-towns, unless there has been an unforeseen event, such as a runway closure, ATC strike or drone presence within the flightpath zones. Wandering through the concourse is a solitary experience, as you realise that the hustle and bustle of the daytime merely masked soullessness. By night, unoccupied and unlit check-in desks stand in silent rows, while airline kiosks are dark and vacant. Tucked away in most terminals are quiet spaces, places of worship, often labelled 'multi-faith'. They are little sanctuaries where, once the door is lightly closed behind you, you can feel a sense of peace and sometimes awe, which is a direct contrast to the crowds outside. I used those rooms from time to time, to get away from the white noise and to find my soul once more. Walking through empty airports in the middle of the night allows you to get a new perspective. You can dream of skateboarding, mountain- biking, BMXing unhindered around the building, or playing hide-and-seek with deadly foes, just like Liam Neeson might have done….(Men, am I on my own here?) Cabin crew and pilots don't live here, nor do ground staff: we all have homes to go to, even if it involves sofa-surfing. I have seen documentaries on people who actually do live in airports and often emerge at night, like a sub-culture, blending in during the day with thousands of others, having constructed rooms behind walls, alongside piping, or in obscure places where they might never be found. They can live for many years undetected… until the BBC catches up with them to make said programmes. The BBC even found a beautiful-looking Middle-Eastern lady whose home is hidden somewhere within the terminal walls of LHR.

There was a room, however, that I often used at a certain airport. It was permanently unlit and contained chairs laid out in the form of beds, with blankets and cushions 'borrowed' from long-haul aircraft, to provide a minimal standard of comfort. In the dark, you could hardly make out anything, except for the electric-green of the security light in the ceiling. I would stay here if it wasn't worth me going home for the night, and I had to be back again in the early morning. It would save me the cost of diesel for a 200 mile round-trip, the risk of falling asleep at the wheel and the fear of being late for work. If I had a daytime flight, I would go back to my car in the afternoon and snooze for a few hours, waiting until about 21:00, before returning to the airport building, so as not to run into anyone I knew.

People ask innocent questions that turn quickly into gossip, and then end up as new rules issued by airlines. I had seen that happen a few times, so I kept myself to myself. The use of this room was permitted and at the same time discouraged, but I reckon that, at its busiest, there could be as many as 20 flight and cabin crew using it at a time. It was so dark in there that it took some adjustment to become aware of a screen which split the room in half, but as far as making out even the person sleeping in the adjacent chair, it was impossible. There were shower rooms on the same level, with an iron and board, hairdryers and closets, and towels you had to sign out, so it wasn't an austere environment. If I couldn't sleep, I would sometimes wander the corridors discreetly, past computers on hot-desks, meeting-rooms, office doors and open-plan areas. Modern airports are a construction marvel, featuring miles of pipework, identical levels, obscure ducts and security cameras. But you see, I too could blend in just like those squatters I mentioned.

Time zones, exhaustion and danger

Such a room was used at a certain U.S. airport for flight crew to sleep in, should they have travelled across the States commuting to their work-duty. Someone put an infra-red camera in there to show how many pilots would use the room: literally as soon as one pilot vacated the bed, there was another climbing in to take his/her place. The reason I mention this is that the investigation into a crash in 2009 of a Colgan Air (Continental) Dash 8 into a town near Buffalo, USA, was probably caused by pilot fatigue leading to an incorrect recovery from a stall-warning. All 49 on board perished. Fatigue – the enemy of the roster. If a pilot or a cabin crew member feels too tired to go to work and wants a lie-in, that's one thing. Pull a sickie (and I've done it on two occasions) and you only have to prove it with a doctor's note. To be unable to work because of exhaustion, brought about by the barely-legal parameters of an airline operation working to rule, is quite different. In the UK, the CAA (Civil Aviation Authority) would be very interested indeed in investigating why this would be happening. In the USA, it would be the FAA (Federal Aviation Authority). A mix of short-haul and long-haul is going to be especially tiring, because of the disruption it causes to the body's Circadian rhythm. Flying back and forth through multiple time-zones is incredibly demanding, and younger cabin crew and pilots fare a little better with this, but not always.

Ironically, it was a short-haul flight to the Czech Republic and back – only an eight hour duty from check-in to check-out – that saw me fall asleep on the motorway a dozen times one summer afternoon. The early setting-off from home at 04:00 didn't help my alertness for the way back. I calculated that my total mileage that day, including commuting, was approximately 1,900 miles. A long-haul duty might be a round-trip, say for JFK (New York) of 6,850 miles – not including commuting. This wasn't one of my routes, but of course I've been there as a pap. On another occasion, I had been delayed returning to LHR from a three-day European trip. The combination of flying, early starts and late finishes coupled to a two hour motorway trip had lulled me into sleep. About 20 minutes from home, after coming off the motorway at 01:30, suddenly a deer leapt across the main road and this is what finally woke me, with a jump akin to a defibrillator shock.

After enduring about a year or so of this blend of domestic, European and transatlantic routes, I finally visited my GP to have a check-up and chat about my own fatigue. I knew I wasn't alone, but this was my story and I couldn't help anyone else, so I helped myself. He didn't think a week off was enough, so he prescribed two weeks off, which instigated some mild quizzing by my manager. As soon as I mentioned the 'fatigue' word, I sensed some backing-off. The rosters for some junior crew, as well as seniors, were punishing all right: back-to-back long haul duties, which in fairness was what some had requested, but with minimum rest in between. Work to live or live to work? That is the question... I was to find out that there was a steady flow of other staff visiting their GPs dotted around the UK, and rightly so. The legal implications bring in Health and Safety Law, an organisation's own policies, and perhaps even an *employer's vicarious liability* for the negligence of its own workers....

So, for all the supposed glamour of being an airline employee, the fact is that it can not only be an incredibly tiring job, but also a lonely and isolated one. What I have found, is that most men and women never admitted to that, almost as if they were too caught up in their preservation of the mystique for the watching world, even their colleagues. Fake smiles, make-up and deportment, are usually the veneers that cover the aching feeling within, that we would all rather be home doing something 'normal' with our loved ones, or even just something mundane, away from work. Sometimes the opposite could be true however, as a few extra hours away might give you time to plough into studies – for example a law degree....

Tokyo, Japan

I used to take my laptop away with me to complete university assignments, using dead-time on stop-overs, while working away from home. One long-haul trip I shouldn't even have been on, but I was to discover that being in Japan intensified my loneliness.

Owing to a car accident at 06:20 just outside of Windsor, and lots of crew arriving late at Heathrow, I was removed from four days of short-haul (ORY and back, MAN and back, PRG and back, given a Nokia to hang around my neck, and ended up being called out within the hour for a Tokyo four-day trip. This was to be a very surreal experience as I was not mentally prepared for going there, plus I was not in charge and the SCCM and I were like chalk and cheese, despite our equivalent rank.

I truly felt far from home – 6,000 miles away – and this was the furthest from England I had ever been. (We had departed at 09.30 from the LHR, crossing many time zones, landing at HAN as the sun was rising at 05.30.) I sat on a bench in Tokyo beside a calming river for hours, opposite an amusement park, watching the world go by, thinking and drawing sketches of what my new business-brand might look like. The hotel was built on rubber owing to earthquakes, and I had mistaken a tremor – which measured eight on the Richter scale – for shenanigans in the room next door. Thankfully, it didn't get any more serious than that while I was there. My hotel room TV's English channels were BBC World News and CNN, both on a loop, with the main headline being the Norwegian terrorist shootings by a local who fancied himself as a Navy Seal. It was a good job I had taken my law books with me, as I completed yet another assessment on constitutional law (yawn!) in the dead-time I had there. Oh – and I bought my first *Krispy Kreme Doughnuts* supplies here and a *McDonalds*

Cheeseburger, making me a truly global consumer. The airport at
HAN (Haneda) was as soulless as any other: a marvel of lighting
and branding, that would appeal to anyone who thinks shopping
centres represent a great day out. I recall that the plane was barely
half-full on the way back to England. Apparently that was always
the way with this route – hardly any one flying ex-Tokyo, owing to
the aftermath of disaster. The previous few months had seen
earthquakes, tsunamis and floods of biblical proportion in Japan,
as documented on global TV reports, and even some of my
colleagues had been stranded there for a few days, escaping with
their lives – and wheelie bags.

The very real threat

There were two airports especially, that you had to be careful with,
and they both happened to be in the continent of Africa: Abuja,
Nigeria (ABV) and Nairobi, Kenya,(NBO) where the terrorist
threat was high. In the case of NBO, an arriving crew, having
made it through customs and the airport concourse, would follow
each other to the crew bus waiting outside to take them to the
hotel, about 15 or 20 minutes away. The bus driver, however,
would switch off the internal lighting, so as not to display its
occupants on the short journey. We would wave goodbye to the
KLM crew in the coach next to us, while they were already on the
'bus-juice' looking merry, and then it was mandatory lights-off
straightaway. An RPG (rocket propelled grenade) or even an

AK-47, would have finished off a crew bus, and a bunch of dead airline crew members would have made international headlines and a trophy-killing for terrorist organisations. Welcome to Africa.

I operated an ABV on the 747-400 once only. These flights were traditionally occupied by many who worked in the oil industry, as Nigeria is rich in oil reserves. It was full to the last seat, and had a payload in Club (J) of about 70 J-class pax. (J is an alternative code letter for C-class). I recall the Nigerian president and other diplomats and dignitaries being on board, travelling in First. It was an uneventful night flight with a difference: we operated the O/B (outbound), with a positioning crew resting upstairs in the upper deck, and changed over for the return flight. It was usually a night stop, but owing to terrorist threats we weren't allowed to stay over, hence the next best option was to take two crews out and swap over on the turnaround at ABV. We therefore didn't even venture past the aircraft doors into the airport. My comment to my crew in the cramped briefing room pre-departure from LHR: "It's too dangerous for you to stay there...but we'll send you there!" As the 747 finally rotated above the lush green grass of ABV and into the sunrise, I braced myself for an explosion which thankfully never happened. My perception of ABV was rooted in the films I had seen as a boy, starring sweaty actors like Roger Moore and Stewart Granger, where bridges, trains and airliners were destroyed by RPG-bearing men in khaki jackets in hot countries. Maybe I should get out more....

Gibraltar

When I did get out more, I was reminded while in GIB (Gibraltar) as 'a civilian' during late 2005, of the SAS shooting of three IRA terrorists in 1988. (We had just returned from Morocco where I had proposed to my wife Helen on the shores of Asilah. It wasn't that romantic, as Ramadan-singing had kept us awake all night, and the land outside our apartment was covered in chicken remains.) The English guy who told us about the shootings seemed to enjoy relaying how the terrorists were dispatched, and had developed a funny look in his eye. Helen and I felt safer as he dropped us off at the airport for our return flight to LHR. The airport there was similar to BRS: built in 1959, with the dated feel of an elderly relative's house – the kind that could do with a serious refit, but still had life in it. They close off the road every time an aircraft lands, as uniquely, the road crosses the runway. Anyway, guess what they did in an almost predictable way? Yes, they fashioned a brand new terminal with all the character and individuality of every other identikit global new-style terminal building with plenty of glass, which opened for inbound traffic in 2011. GIB was served by Monarch until it went under, as described in Chapter Five, and that airline used to be responsible for about a third of the traffic at GIB. Don't worry, though, because full of heart, Easyjet quickly stepped in to take over the slots. The approach to GIB is a marvel, owing to the dramatic backdrop of the world-famous 'Rock', and is apparently subject to unusual wind-patterns/gusts caused by the rock, but it seemed fine to me. A word of warning though: have nothing to do with the Barbary apes that you'll encounter if you venture up the Rock. They're thieving little parasites who'll urinate on you if they take a shine to your jacket. Pass the wet-wipes please.

Beirut, Lebanon

Dramatic for another reason was BEY (Beirut, Lebanon), which I visited again as 'a civilian' three times in the early 2000s. For those of you who have never been to the country, it is simply beautiful, sitting on the edge of the Mediterranean with a rich heritage. A friend of mine once said, "Welcome to the land of olives and automatic weapons!" The airport has three runways, and was always welcoming and well-run whenever I passed through using either BA (British Mediterranean) or MEA (Middle East Airlines). In 2006, all that changed after an Israeli Air Force attack which destroyed the use of the runways, and caused an evacuation of Westerners, mainly via the port. There was a feeling of both sadness and relief whenever I took off from BEY, especially if travelling alone. This was a combination of the happy memories and being in a place that had such a bad reputation for war. I hope to revisit one day as the olives were amazing, and so was the hospitality. However, there were bullet holes in a fair few buildings, as well as the collateral damage of past missile bombardment, which I saw at first hand in the quaint and thriving port city of Tyre, as well as in Beirut itself.

Harare, Zimbabwe

I ventured into HRE (Harare, Zimbabwe) in 2002, on an orphanage visit with some friends. What struck me most on arrival, was how busy the airport was, and how prominently Robert Mugabe's portraits were placed. (You couldn't draw a moustache on them as he already had one.) I suffered some insults from a young man who took offence at my presence – a rich Westerner coming around to take photographs of a family in the slums. I have a shot of a mother with three children around her: little did I realise that she would soon lose her youngest babe-in-arms to HIV. James, Big-Rich and I had gone there for a ten-day humanitarian trip to deliver hygiene supplies, sports goods, clothing and general aid. Whilst we were there, we were deployed to a couple of orphan-feeding projects to give advice on various aspects of health and safety, build basketball hoops and football goals, attend church meetings, and give general assistance where needed. Rich and I also ended up visiting an orphanage full of HIV-infected kids who would probably never know the security and love of a family. I held a little blind boy in my arms, which nearly broke my heart as his little head rested on my shoulder. On arrival, all I had to do was just look at a group of kids with a glint in my eye, and within about ten seconds I had a group of about a dozen seven-year-olds chasing me around the complex. I don't know who found it more fun – me or them. It ended up with me being thumped in the balls by all of them, but I guess that's where excitement takes you. I had also managed to block the toilet a couple of times at our hosts' home, leaving Rich to take the blame: it was more amusing that way.

A couple of days before we were due to leave, our hosts Keith and Kathy informed us that Keith had to go to his brother's farm and collect all the equipment he could, as Mugabe had sent instructions to his 'war-veterans' (thugs with handguns) to commandeer all white-owned land and plunder it. Later that evening, with the sun going down, we could only then appreciate the magnitude of what Keith had done when we watched around 30 flat-bed HGV's drove up laden with pipes, equipment and machinery, pull up right outside their home. Keith had actually had a gun pulled on him, but had diffused the situation.

Unbeknown to us, Rich had not had a comfortable flight over and had been praying for better seats on our return to the UK. As we checked in at the BA desk, 5,000 miles away from home, I recognised a former flying colleague from LGW as the duty manager: I had been the No.1 on her first ever flight as a C/A four years earlier. Ellie took our boarding passes, scrubbed out our M (Economy) reservations, and gracefully gave us three seats in Club, so Harare to London was a much more comfortable experience. I led my friends to the Club lounge where they were astounded at my confidence in raiding the free supplies. Up in the air, as I held out my third glass of Port, the irony was not lost on me: God had answered Rich's prayers and we were flying away in luxury, while most of the native Africans we left behind, had precious little. We came back tanned from the African sun, more than a little enlightened, and much more appreciative of what we had.

Saddam International, Iraq

I can't really *not* tell you about this, as it was such a thrilling yet surreal moment to be landing in Mesopotamia, "the birthplace of civilisation", along with Hungary, Italy, Greece and Israel all claiming the same accolade. It was July 2003, and the Americans had seized control of the capital and the airport too, with the military might of a well-executed campaign. The approach took us over 1000's of square miles of Iraq's desert sands, barren fields, and palm trees as we got nearer to the runway threshold. I felt a little emotional as the AirServ King Air turboprop touched down at SDA (Saddam International), thinking how comparatively few westerners would ever have been in my position. On taxiing in, we passed a couple of redundant Iraqi Airways Boeings, tens of Blackhawk helicopters, a few Hercules C-130's and several C-17 Globemaster transporters. The airfield was rapidly renamed BGW (Baghdad International Airport) under IATA (Internal Air Transport Association) codes to dissociate any connection with Saddam Hussein, and was situated about ten miles out of the capital city. As I explained earlier on in the book, the heat that rushed in was unbearable when the aircraft doors were finally opened by the F/O. It was exactly as you might imagine Shadrach, Meschach and Abednego in the furnace of King Nebuchadnezzar, the monarch of Babylon (current-day Iraq). Accompanied by armed US soldiers, we walked away from the aircraft towards the complex, but it was the dry baking heat that was all we could think about. We were escorted by soldiers into a large hangar where we were all questioned extensively about the purpose of our visit, searched along with our bags, passports checked and our names recorded on computer, before being allowed to leave the airport building. Outside, a United Nations coach was waiting to collect us. As I understood it, there were two flights daily operated on behalf of the UN between BGW and Amman. We were also a sitting duck for snipers, anti-aircraft guns and RPGs. (No matter which way I turn I can't seem to get away from RPGs.) I was never to see the airport again, as we were to return to Jordan by road. I would of course been happier to fly, even though there was no in-flight service, after all, this was post-war, but only just....

On a happier note, contrast BGW with quieter airports like RTM (Rotterdam) or ANT (Antwerp), where the ground staff could sometimes happily leave you alone if you were on a N/S (night-stop) and organise the hotel pick-up for a little later. I was once the victim of a 'lock-in' at ANT, where instead of vacating the ATR about ten minutes after the last pax, we stayed on for about an hour while the drinks trolley remained open. Put it this way, I had a fondness for G&T, gin and bitter lemon, and Piper Heidseck quarter bottles, and the captain was no better. Once the four of us had shut up shop, the aircraft was locked up for the night with the props secured, and we were back at the hotel, a business man whom none of us had ever met before, bought us all a further bottle of Champagne. I can't remember the reason he did this, but the next day I had one of the best headaches that I had ever endured. So did the other three. You had to know which crew members you could trust on split-duty night stops, but it seemed to work well enough in principle. A split-duty was the nearest thing you'd get to 'a jolly', so it was wise to take full advantage of the bar trolley, just like they did in the old days. No wonder crew are smiley.

Nigel the cleaner

Under cover of evening darkness, a friend of mine, Nigel, who was an airport cleaner at North Terminal at the time, used to clean a certain US carrier's executive lounge. At around 9 or 10pm one night, he got talking to a couple who had missed their flight to the States and were in need of some consolation. *"What would Jesus do?"* He asked them to wait, and disappeared for a few moments. He simply went behind the desk, helped himself to a couple of invitations to the executive lounge, reserved for premium pax, and returned handing them to the now deeply-impressed couple with his compliments on behalf of the airline, his bucket still in his hand. Now that's what I call customer service. Nigel was the most over-qualified broom-pusher there. He would later announce to us without warning, that he was leaving LGW to join a ship in the North Sea, and was to be flown up by BA to Scotland the next day. He now oversees undersea pipe-laying all over the world, especially off Nigeria, Norway and in the Middle East. He was – and is – a trained hydrographic surveyor. He's older now with family responsibilities, but I think he still carries a bucket everywhere.

Upgrades

In a similar fashion, I was always the one up for upgrading deserving-people, handing out flatbeds, or simply larger seats in short-haul, like sweeties. Ah, upgrades: you were probably wondering when I would touch on this hallowed subject. I was operating an NBO inbound to LHR one night and I ventured into the flight deck five hours in, to do my usual cabin report. Amit the SFO turned around to me to ask how it was going back there. I replied, "It's fine… actually, I've just upgraded eight people!"

Amit: "What's your name? Father Christmas?!"

I responded: "No… Robin Hood!"

And that's exactly who I felt like in those moments. On that particular flight, I had bumped up five belonging to a Premier card holder's family, so the commercial decision was strategic. I can't recall why I upgraded the rest to Club World, but they all smiled gratefully. On one flight I operated, a pretty girl in her 20s, smartly-dressed came on board the 777 last, looking slightly like a film-star, and, in an upper-class English accent, asked us the direct question, "Could I have an upgrade, please?" I looked at her and simply said, "I have to have a very good commercial reason to do so." She frowned slightly and turned towards the rear of the aircraft, without arguing. I didn't mind her asking, as she was daring enough to do so, and it was obvious she had done so before, hence deliberately coming on last. Other people would ask the same if they happened to see spare seats in Club. The same answer was given.

I would do it on a case-by-case basis if there was capacity – and it made sense to do so for example if businesspeople or families especially were split apart. Sometimes, it might be Executive Club pax who had endured lengthy journeys with problems along the way, especially if they were nice and reasonable about the request. I once upgraded a deportee travelling from Dublin. I don't think he could believe his luck when I offered him a glass of bubbly. Nice to make someone's journey a little more special where possible. You simply checked the paperwork: the pax list showing TOB (total on board), special requests, edits and comments, which also showed spare seat locations across all the cabins. One time I saw an old school-mate, and thought it would make his experience better. That was a one-off, as there was blatantly no commercial reason whatsoever for giving him a Club seat, unless BA needed a house built one day.

You've got to think about the bigger picture, and to me upgrading was just a tool to help, not only straightaway to remedy a problem, but in the longer-term, the positive impact might be felt for years afterwards. You give away a comfy seat, and a traveller might remember that act for a longtime to come, and the benefit for the airline is that he or she will be ten times more likely to recommend that airline to others, and remain fiercely loyal to the brand. It works for so many other areas of life. Think about it – wouldn't you do the same? That said, I can't think of anyone in my position who ever bothered filling out the official paperwork, as there simply wasn't time on board. Just get everyone seated, close up and get going. Delays don't win anyone prizes, but an early-close wins the captain's favour. Call it the dispatcher in me....

Chapter Nine

Return to base

Being out of an industry for 11 years can make you feel like a fish out of water on returning, and once settled, make you doubt why you ever returned at all. Something had happened in those 11 years, that would alter the perception of commercial flying for both insiders and outsiders. Yes, I nearly made it with my band – the first in the world to do the 'dancing stormtroopers' video, before others got on the bandwagon and I subsequently got married to my beautiful wife. Oh sorry, *that* world-changing event: I will expand on this later on. However, when you need a job you need a job, and you have to play to your strengths, or at least invent new ones. A friend had asked the Reluctant Air Steward years earlier, if he would ever go back to it, and our man had replied, "Only if BA offer direct-entry senior roles, and that will probably never happen…." At random one day, the Reluctant Air Steward found and went for the Customer Service Manager (CSM) role online, where it promised that the application would take around 40 minutes. It actually took four days to complete properly.

Our man was successful in being offered an interview/ assessment day, and trekked up to LHR, leaving his Wiltshire home at 02:30 by bicycle in the freezing November air, to catch an 03:25 coach, arriving at LHR 05:30. His suit carrier in hand, he changed in a toilet cubicle at Terminal One, whilst the Eastern European man shaving at a nearby basin, erupted with laughter as he witnessed the transformation of a scruff-bag into a passable impression of an executive. From there, he caught a tube to Hatton Cross and then onto Cranebank, where he knocked on the window of the security shelter, making the female guard jump as he was so early. He was ahead of the staff opening up the recruitment block by 20 minutes, and was let inside to sit at one of the tables. One by one, fellow applicants in their late 20s through to their late 40s came through the door, and as the nested 'executive' listened in to conversations, small-talk, voice-timbres and accents, he began to realise how strange it was being back in this world....

The assessment started at 08.00 with the weights, heights and arm-reaches of all the candidates being taken. There were four exercises: a written test, a 'deeply-unhappy pax' scenario, a boardroom setting to observe how you made and explained decisions and interacted with others, and finally a two-to-one interview, where the probing started. It was a grilling on how you would deal with insubordination, unfairness, expectations and morale.

Treating himself to an overpriced KitKat Chunky from the vending machine, our man called his wife at 13:00 to tell her the assessment was over, that he had done his best but felt it wasn't good enough, and was shortly to resume his long journey home. The next day, about his duties as an agency chef, he received a couple of 'withheld number' calls, which he dismissed as probably being his dad, or most likely the catering agency, but definitely not the airline. Mobiles were frowned upon by the assignment boss so, discreetly, he took the phone into the office and listened hard to the voicemail. His smile widened and he whispered to himself, "At last! Something's going right...." He had been selected as a Customer Service Manager for the national carrier. This time, there was no Labrador to cry alongside him, and of course you will know, dear reader – by him, I mean me.

The training course was a six-week affair, which meant a meeting with the bank to persuade them to lend me a couple of grand to cover a vehicle, living expenses and bills for that period. I was toying with the idea of a motorhome, but the only ones I could afford were ancient petrol ones and totally uneconomical. Once in, my heartstrings were tugged, as I was begged not to go, but I had to. It needed to be on my CV that I was back in the job market acquiring updated skills. In truth, I felt lost and blown about by the wind, like a bruised reed. I didn't know whether accepting the job was the right thing to do or not. There were to be 16 delegates on my course, and I was the only one with young children, still married and with the longest commute. I was far from home, and spent the first two nights in a tent at a campsite, six miles or so from LHR. Two of my mates came to keep me company on the second evening, and marvelled at my electric hook-up and radio inside the tent. Paul commented that it gave new meaning to the term 'camp steward' and continued to eye up my storm-pegs, while Malcolm shook his head and bought the burgers.

Throughout the rest of the training course, I stayed in a cheap hostel in Northwoods, near Ealing. It had dormitories with bunk beds, a shared kitchen with a dated feel, leaking bathrooms, and overall was in poor condition. It was, however, a roof over my head, plus I met many interesting characters there, for the male camaraderie and diversity was strong. I didn't tell my course colleagues about any of this, as they would have looked at me as if I was the black sheep, and almost certainly would have moved their seats away from mine. 25% of us would leave within just 18 months of joining. (Thinking to myself that it was no big deal that I had been selected, a colleague put me right: "That selection day you went on, seven CSM's were chosen, but whole other days could go past with *no-one* getting through. You've done bloody well to get in, Simon!") During the six weeks, a couple of the boys gave themselves nicknames like *Princess* and *Muscles* and acted out *Steps* dance routines. The girls seemed a little more refined. I asked our trainer, Marie-Claire – (she was 83 pages long!) – what her biggest tip was for a long-haul SCCM. Her reply was: "A sense of humour". I took that with me as I left my training course, feeling like the odd one out, as I looked around at my colleagues who were fresh from other airlines, whereas I had been out of the industry for so long. She told me that it was obvious I had struggled through the course, and she was right. My mind was elsewhere, and I wasn't as bothered as others that we were being treated like kids on the training course. Like all cabin crew and pilots, I was itching to get out of the training room and actually do what I was paid for. My job was to provide for my family.

In safe hands

My first flying duty for British Airways mainline, after the Pisa familiarisation-flight, should have been a 'there-and-back' to TIP (Tripoli, Libya), but the route was suspended owing to 'serious threats to security' – ie, being shot out of the sky by RPGs (rocket-propelled grenades). Instead, my next duty was to be LAS (Las Vegas), my first long-haul experience as an in-charge SCCM on a wide bodied aircraft type I had not flown on before – the Boeing 777 ('The Triple-Seven'). I had that same uncertain feeling you have on your first day in a new job, but with 300 people relying on you knowing what you're doing, including a team waiting to pick holes in your leadership. No pressure, then....

Having checked in at CRC (Crew Report Centre), I introduced myself and shook hands with the three flight crew outside the briefing room, but it was the captain who seemed strangely familiar. I continued to brief my new-found crew whom I haven't forgotten to this day, owing to their support and good-humour on this trip. One of the older girls, an ex-painter and decorator, said to me as we walked through the terminal along an endless concourse past hordes of travellers and tax-free shops:

"You're very calm for your first flight." My outward appearance belied the extreme anxiety I was busy suppressing. It took me the full 20 minutes to commute to the B-gates of T5, to find our departure gate, board the enormous 777-200 and to process who this familiar-looking man might be. I found him inside the plane waiting to use the toilet. "I know who you are…" I said to him, as he smiled back at me, "…the incident-man." (I had remembered his heroic face on all the front pages, pictured with his team.)

A few hours later, once all the occupants had been fed and watered, I sent my first team upstairs to the bunks for their break, while I disappeared into the flight deck to have a prolonged chat with the guys at the sharp end. Actually it was always a great excuse for CRM (Crew Resource Management – rapport and bonding) as well as the chance to look out the pilots' windows at the ice-pyramids of Greenland, play chase with other airliners and marvel at the flying systems. The captain, along with his team on a routine day in 2010, had skilfully – and without fatality to anyone on board, crash-landed a giant – exactly the same as we were flying – just short of the runway at LHR. I will leave you to look up the details online, suffice to say that he and I and the SF/O (Senior First Officer) flying the route to LAS had a lengthy talk about how the whole accident was handled after the event. During the official investigation, he felt ostracised once back at work, to the extent that other personnel would leave him to eat his lunch alone. That's how heroes are treated. His wife meanwhile had helped transform his life with a book and a side-hustle as a motivational speaker. (The accident was caused by ice blocking the fuel oil heat exchanger and was a design fault in the engine, which was rectified by Rolls Royce.)

He and the SF/O were very encouraging to me and listened to my story – we all have one, and I have learnt that mine is just as important as yours – and it turned my first sector out to the USA into a very pleasant experience. It dawned on me as I left the flight deck to resume cabin patrol, that God had reminded me of something: "*I'm always with you- you're in safe hands.*" I was in charge of the cabin crew in an airliner flying at 41,000ft, lips as dry as a mountaineer's, feeling like an outsider to an industry I had left a decade earlier, and, considering the randomness of the situation I had been given the safest physical hands possible: the captain who had defied calamity.

What next? We er... landed, did the usual cabin checks, welcomed on an army of cleaners, caterers and engineers, then left the aircraft ourselves. I soon found myself in a short customs and clearance queue for 'Crew' which seemed to last an age. Long-haul arrivals make your body feel as though it has just been subject to a battering by a baseball bat, coupled with the feeling of being 'zoned-out'. We got to the hotel, had a few drinks and I went to bed with enough pillows for a king.

I was soon to find out that crews can sometimes be offered breakfast deals that could set you up for the day, depending on how accommodating the hotel felt towards the block-room-booking airline. It really is hit-and-miss sometimes, whether you will actually eat while up in the air or whether there is a contractual provision for the airline to provide crew-food while on duty, either in the air or on terra-firma. Sometimes, you survive on whatever snacks you can find in the drinks trolleys. The most amazing food selection I ever saw on offer was at a grand hotel in Antwerp in the Nineties: wall-to-wall mirrors which reflected an array of fresh pineapples, grapefruit, mango, and other exotic fruits, to sausages, four types of cooked eggs, pastries, croissants, cereals and so on.... The downer was that we only had ten minutes in which to eat before the crew bus came, but in those precious moments you felt like an intruder in a palace.

Let me take you back to the story of my return leg from Las Vegas, 24 hours after I had landed.... We were with a different set of pilots now, having left the outbound flight crew behind at the hotel, as they had a proper stopover as opposed to our minimum rest. As we arrived back at McCarran International, the last of my crew members – a quiet chap in his late 30s – got out of the bus, and threw up discreetly into a planter by the roadside. Immediately, the ageing-captain pounced, and told me that this guy would have to stay at LAS, as he wasn't "fit for duty, and the 'JPM' (Operations Manual) stated the same in black and white". It took all my powers of persuasion to convince him that we could carry him, and continue the service without him safely enough, allowing him time to rest. What would be the point of leaving him over 5,000 miles from home? The commander continued his line of argument that he was either fit to fly or not, and eventually backed down, mumbling something about flight rules.

The night-flight went fine, and the captain turned out to be quite genial, with the patient re-joining us in the morning for the breakfast service. We prepared the cabin for landing at 40 minutes to go and, back at LHR, disbanded by the baggage carousel at about 15:00. I will never forget the cheerful and supportive characters who made up my first long-haul flight. I didn't bother filling out a Flight Incident Report to cover my colleague's sickness, as I didn't deem it necessary.

Fast forward a few days, and, on checking-in for my next duty, a new Red Notice in the mandatory safety-updates file, highlighted the importance of filling in a safety-incident report, specifically for crew sickness down route. This had gone out to about 17,000 colleagues at LHR alone, and you can bet it was the same captain who had obviously checked that whether or not I had done this, and gone one stage further by reporting it. Lesson learned: cover your back – be it by an email trail or paperwork filled in – as there's always someone waiting for you to trip, or to help trip you up themselves.

Stand up for yourself, and others

ATL (Atlanta) was a prestigious route, if only because it was used by Coca-Cola chief executives who had given BA their allegiance via corporate contract, to fly them back and forth across the Atlantic. On my first ATL, something happened that broke the unity of my colleagues working at the rear of the 777. Several of my crew members were ex-temps having been brought in and out of seasonal employment over the previous couple of years, and were therefore experienced in delivering the cabin service. Some I worked with had obvious 'chips on their shoulders', not only with their immediate colleagues, but also with those of a higher rank. One particular junior steward had caused such vexation to my lot down the back, by ordering them about and attempting to bully them, that my No.2 – a stewardess – called me the following day at the hotel to say 'thanks, but no thanks' to my offer of allowing her to operate as the SCCM on the return flight. (This was customary for many SCCM's to allow No.2 C/As the chance to gain some experience 'operating up' in advance of promotion.) She thought it best to to remain as she was, and to look after a situation that had developed with a particular steward not-so-subtly throwing his weight around, undermining everyone else. As it happened, he was well-built.

The I/B flight fared no better, as described by one of my immediate colleagues, Tom, who complained of him bashing carts, throwing keys around and swearing within earshot of the pax. Flustered, he made a beeline for me while I was patrolling the cabin at 03:00. Seeing his anguish and also clocking the 'perpetrator' on a diagonal line looking at me from Door 4R, I smiled at him in the obscurity of the darkened cabin, as he said: "Simon, could I talk to you?" I simply replied, "Tom, keep looking at me and don't look anywhere else – it's all right – I know."

"You know?!"

"Of course I know…". (I rarely knew anything, so this was a revelation to me: to actually know something ahead of a few others.)

I gave Tom the options to feed back to the others. Option One: "I deal with the bully straightaway." (I am not a particular fan of confrontation, but even I recognise it has to be done every now and then to enforce your standpoint.) Option Two: "With only five hours of the flight left, to leave it, as we all might never work with the guy again." (A weak choice as it doesn't deal with the problem.) Option Three: "Leave it for now, and let me deal with it properly back at base." They all chose the last option, so I emailed his base-manager on return and stuck up for my crew. This action unbelievably curtailed at last, a history of abusive behaviour that had been allowed to drag on for months.

This taught me a big lesson: even though conflict hurts, you have to deal with it and not shy away from it but I'm still not sure I handled it as well as I could have done. What happened to the guy with the bullying behaviours? Well, even though I had no problem with him personally, during the flight he obviously had one with me, as he told me he had been a senior before: "I've had the silver tie before, mate.…". His struggles seemed to be with himself, and he was taken off-duty for a while. Mental health is something we should *all* take care of and my guess is that he struggled with his identity in this rarefied world, and was probably just as much a reluctant air steward as myself. That episode caused me to treat long-haul flights especially, in a different fashion. With up to 16 cabin crew on some flights and around 300 punters, coupled with the traversing of maybe 5,000 miles, there was more to go wrong. Team cohesion was vital, and it all goes back to my comments in Chapter Seven about the impact of seniors on a flight. Get this bit right and it'll go well: make your expectations clear and value – *truly value* – your co-workers, because you never know when you might need their expertise....

Another world

I was introduced to the worlds of First Class and Club World while working at LHR. Not that I had never been aware of them, but working in both was a little bit of an eye-opener at first. If you are wondering what goes on behind that curtain, and then the other curtain beyond that one, it's like another microcosm. The first thing you notice is the seat-layout and the sizes of everything: Flat beds, luxurious leather, bright colours, personal mood lighting, large touchscreen TVs, silver buttons, privacy screens and, crucially, space. These features are mostly common to both cabins, and the return on investment for an airline is enormous. As I've said before, 14 occupied seats in First at the front of a Boeing 747-400 might bring in a return-trip income of around £150,000 alone. That's a significant contribution to the coffers. When you think that the airline had 50 or more 747-400s while I was there, then you can start thinking about the daily mathematics of the First Class operation alone. Look after the premium pax and they'll look after the airline. However if they find a better deal, or have a disappointment on one or more flights, they'll switch as easily as you might do between utility providers. Do they get spoiled onboard? Hmmm, let's just say they fly as frequently as air-crew themselves, so they know instinctively what they are entitled to and how a service should run. (Like a more advanced version of me, who would order a coffee on a 40-minute Greek Aegean flight, only because it came with a massive chocolate cookie. You see – I knew the system.) Premium customers pay heavily for being spoilt, but as I have explained previously, it's as much for their ticket flexibility as the flat bed and attentive, customised service with their own 'flight-plan' dictating how they want their service to run in First.

The First galley on the Triple and the Jumbo impressed me for several reasons: it had wine coolers, warming ovens for nuts and a Nespresso capsule machine as well as the usual stowages. There was a wardrobe at the front, while the toilets had fake flowers that were sprayed with special air freshener. Freebies for both classes included exclusive wash-bags, amenity kits, slippers and socks, plus logo'd blankets the quality of which improved the further you went towards the front of the plane. Even the Champagne quality went way up the scale – *Laurent Perrier Grand Siecle (NV)*, retailing at around £130 a bottle. Did I sample it? Not in the air. Let's just say we have time-honoured tricks and I'm not giving them away here… and yes, if you drink it too quickly, the bubbles go up your nose, in the same way as a can of Tango. (Say, this guy's classy….)

Crew rest areas for long haul crew members were located at the rear of the 747 by Doors 5, and via an anonymous-looking door at 3R on the 777. Up the ladder on the latter and you were into the part of the plane affectionately known as the 'coffins' area – long, body-length tubes positioned side by side (or in bunkbeds on the jumbo), individually curtained-off, each with a pillow, sleeping bag and safety belt for turbulence. Ideal for a couple of hours crude sleep, with the background air-con and miscellaneous aircraft noise to lull you into the sensation of rest. When you wake, you'll feel (and look) arguably worse than when you entered this domain, leaving you ripe for the last hour or two of in-flight service, before landing.

Coffins and the unexplained...

I mentioned coffins just then, and there is a story that I was told on the bus going from the hotel to Lisbon airport (LIS), Portugal, and it gave me the chills. I found out afterwards that every airline has their own version, but it goes something like this....

A C/A goes to the rear of the jumbo, hears crying coming from the crew rest area and finds a lady pap crying there. She tells her that she shouldn't be there, but the lady ignores her. The C/A tries to console her, and tactfully attempts to move her away but the lady manages to say: "Please tell my husband it's all right – I'm here. I'm okay... he's seated in 23A...." The C/A tells the lady she has to leave the area, but she will let her husband know. She walks down the cabin to find the gentleman in 23A, and tells him she has a message from his wife to tell him that she's okay. "My wife?" says the man, puzzled…. "My wife has died. She's in the hold." It made me rethink the idea of going to the crew rest area alone on the jumbo, but I was able to leap out on unsuspecting female colleagues, provoking shrieks and a little blue language. I could be just as jumpy, but a couple of mini-KitKats from the rear galley pax snack boxes could sedate me just fine.

I did hear from another colleague a story that required further investigation on the internet. Fiona had been working a long-haul night-flight a couple of years earlier and had been taking her rest in a C-class seat. She had the sensation of being slapped in the face, and woke up immediately to see no-one there. On the same flight she found out that the F/O had had a similar experience, while sat sleeping in a seat at the rear of the First Class cabin. He found himself being forcibly pinned to his seat and knocked about before being released by an unseen presence. His ID pass strap, which was normally neatly wound around the photo was strewn in the tray next to him. Both of them were quite freaked out understandably. I put two and two together, and wondered if the plane had been on an African run, as many planes are used on the same rotation, owing to scheduling. My research showed a possible link: In 2010, a man had been deported to Angola, and was suffocated by over-zealous security guards, which was distressing for the witnesses to the event – the nearby pax. The plane operating BA77 never even took off from LHR. What if this aircraft held a secret…? You may recall an earlier reference in chapter four, 'Terror in the Skies', to an Eastern Airlines L1011 which crashed in the Everglades swamps...? Parts of the recovered aircraft were later used as spares for other L1011s on the same fleet, and it was then that some very disturbing events took place, with deceased flight-crew appearing to crew and pax alike on those aircraft. They even made a film about it starring Ernest Borgnine – (remember the old helicopter pilot in *Airwolf*?!) Planes can be creepy environments.

The power of confectionery

I found that my kids liked me better when I returned from a long haul trip if only because they knew I would be loaded with... chocolate. "Daddy's back!" they would yell, when my little red Fiesta would appear up the road, flashing and steering erratically. They knew what Daddy's return meant, the little scavengers. Ah, chocolate: that ancient bargaining tool, which, for decades since WW2, has ensured that children's highs are high, and vice versa. I would get them to clear a space on the kitchen table, before theatrically turning out my bag, spilling out around 28 bars of mixed confectionery to grabbing little hands.

On that subject, the Hilton at PHX (Phoenix, Arizona) had a free M&M's dispenser at reception. I wondered how I could transport a load back for the kids and it dawned on me, as I recalled a scene from *The Great Escape*, that I could convey them up to my room in stages. In the film, they were getting rid of sandbags down their trouser-legs. Here, I was doing the reverse: I was transporting small containers at the reception desk up to my room to fill two disposable coffee cups with lids. They must have wondered why I made quite so many trips down to reception, but the plan worked. Back at home, predictably, the children went hyper and my wife told me off, mainly because I had tried to dispense the sweets down my trousers just like Dickie Attenborough and Steve McQueen. You have to ask yourself if it was ever worth it and I say it was, for the sheer audacity of it. As opposed to my childless colleagues, I couldn't retire to bed after flying duties, as I would be needed for kids' duties. Not even a chance of two slices of cucumber for my eyes.

There were the odd moments of peace on trips where, during those 'rest-periods' (i.e. between-flights), I could get out of the hotel and go exploring. My favourite destination of all was probably SAN (San Diego), if only for the fantastic weather and the proximity of a decommissioned aircraft carrier within a mile. I remember walking through the sunny streets for hours and buying my wife a jewelled watch as an anniversary present, crossing tramlines and being mesmerised by the famous giant statue of a sailor embracing his girlfriend, with a Bob Hope monologue on repeat through the speakers. The Christmas market at the square in Budapest, Hungary, brings back a vivid memory of the smell of cinnamon and spices in the mulled wine aroma that drifted sweetly across the cold December evening sky. (I still owe the captain Andy for buying me a meal when I couldn't get any cash out. Andy happened to be that F/O from my Banjul trip with 'Hawkeyes' all those years earlier....) I would make use of the swimming pools whenever I could if I was on a European night-stop, while the Jacuzzi in our hotel at downtown Denver, was truly the most relaxing experience after a battering 11-hour flight from the UK, and you could almost fall asleep in it. Long-haul: it's just as tiring for crew as it is for pax.

Are you serious?

The serious side of flying was very much in evidence throughout this time because of 9/11. During our earlier training at Cranebank, we had been ushered through the obligatory safety and survival phases. The hijacking scenario was in the 737 cabin mock-up, and we were told to treat it absolutely seriously. One of the trainers – an old guy, who was almost certainly ex-special forces or CO19 (Armed police unit) – played the hooded hijacker with a large handgun, shouting at us: "Get your 'f***ing heads down!!'" The cabin lights suddenly went off and a loud voice commanded the situation from there. As I took the brace-type position, with my heart beating a little quicker, I thought I could rush him just for the hell of it, and was on the verge of doing so, but simply because I knew it would be over in ten minutes, I let it carry on. Renald and a couple of the girls would probably have grabbed me anyway. My reasoning was that if hijackers were going to take over an A/C, what would stop them from doing what they did in spectacular fashion all those years earlier? "Me" was the answer in my head. Oh, and a sky-marshal. We were told during our training that there would always be one on-board, but he would never reveal himself to the crew. I gave up trying to be an amateur sleuth and trying to figure out who the sky marshal was. With all the cuts and savings that organisations are forced to make in both public and private sectors, I concluded that it could have just been a reassuring training-line that we were given.

Online, there was a tangible undertow on pretty much every flight – including the shortest domestic ones – that something could happen. We had special flight-deck door-opening procedures and codes to punch in, before the door could be unlocked from the inside, subject to CCTV clearance from the boys upfront. Even something as ordinary as bringing in meal trays and drinks to the flight deck, required us to look up at the camera after keying in the code and checking that the galley area was clear of any pax, usually helped by a drawn curtain. During training, Marie-Claire had told us that should you punch in the entry code, and the pilots look back at the CCTV screen to check the coast is clear, and see you with a man holding a knife to your throat, they will do the following: they will quietly switch off the camera, turn back to their controls and resume flying the aircraft, according to their brief. That was a chilling reminder that we were effectively segregated from support and were on our own. Understandable, yet chilling nonetheless. Talking of which....

My thoughts on 9/11

I, like most of my colleagues, completely accepted the official narrative of those world-changing events until quite recently, when I started to look at YouTube videos, and read 'alternative' explanations and reports. As a result, I can now no longer watch my *Flight 93* DVD. I looked at it at first from an airline insider's perspective, knowing how airliners work and how the routines go. Then I examined the wider picture. Here's my brief run-down: at the time, cell-phone technology did not allow calls to be made from A/C over 10,000ft maximum. This was proved in a subsequent experiment from a light aircraft. Officially, we were told that crystal-clear calls during the hijacks were made from heights of around 30,000ft (FL 300.) Several of the calls did not match up to the 'hijacking' times. One of the calls from a C/A was analysed, and after the phone message was delivered, the line was left open: these whispered words were clearly audible: "It's a frame…"

The official departure records for that day apparently had no take-off times record of at least two of the flights from the airports concerned. This is an interesting point indeed. It is practically unthinkable that a couple of departures' rotation times could be missed off the list.

The Boeing add-on called a 'flight termination system' allows remote controlled flying from the ground in a 'hijacking scenario'. It also turns off transponders.

The buildings, when designed, were specifically designed to take the impact of Boeing 707 aircraft and remain intact. A retired training captain, John Lear, took several highly experienced pilots into the 767 sim to test out their abilities to fly a course as per that day. None of them could manage it at the high speeds of around 500 knots, and he only managed it himself by reducing to landing speed of circa 150 knots. His conclusion: It is impossible for captains with these Boeing aircraft type-ratings to control sophisticated modern 757/767 airliners at the purported speeds and heights so as to manoeuvre them into a course for a target, let alone barely-trained Cessna pilots, as we were told the hijackers were. The physical stresses alone could cause an airframe to break up ahead of its target. Concrete and steel girders will crumple an aluminium/titanium airframe on impact – see the YouTube video of an F4 Phantom being propelled into a brick wall and the results. Remember, a frozen bird can bring an airplane down.

There was no evidence at all for an airliner being flown into the Pentagon, no wreckage of a plane. The crater where Flight 93 was supposed to have been buried was visible on Google Earth pictures in 1996. No wreckage was dug up, but apparently engines and panels 'were blown away'. (Must have been some wind to blow thousands of tons of metal away into the atmosphere with no trace.) The 'tin kickers' (investigators) were also denied initial access. The FBI weren't, and 'found' Arab passports. Eye-witnesses at New York would have heard the earth-shattering volume of a jet approaching long before impact, as it would have been about 130 decibels at the purported heights and speeds, yet nothing was heard at all. Eye witnesses saw an airliner shape but didn't see any logos, and described them as "grey, with no windows, almost like a military jet." Drones and hologram technology have been in existence for three decades. I will leave the ACARS (flight-deck text-messaging system) evidence, which shows two 'crashed' aircraft still transmitting their signals hundreds of miles away, *after* the impacts. Oh, did I forget to mention the clearing of all personnel from a certain US air force base a couple of hours before the impacts hit the news? Silly me.

Obviously, keep an open mind and draw your own conclusions, but I hope that the facts above alone might make you scratch your head and encourage you to research them for yourself. You may well know about all of this anyway. There is far more that I haven't mentioned here. I kicked myself as an airline employee for not looking at this in greater detail far earlier. I have been disappointed that a couple of my ex-colleagues, including a captain and a flight technical-records manager, think that I'm just a conspiracy theorist, and should probably go to bed with a hot mug of cocoa. Maybe I should, but I have to put my own kids to bed first, plus, drinking anything past 6pm makes me get up in the night....

My personal conclusion is that the whole event was a component part of something more sinister. Were the airlines in on it? At executive level, I don't think they were given a choice. I'm not the only one who is convinced the day was staged. I defended the allied invasion of Iraq in 2003 if only to get rid of Sadaam. Now, I see 9/11 was the perfect 'excuse' to secure the oil fields for western consumption. There are deeper threads that unravel a far more disturbing picture of the western world we think is so safe. Our leaders are not necessarily 'the good guys'. (See the story of BA149 in August 1990, landing at Kuwait City two hours *after* the Iraqi invasion, when the crew was supposed to be warned if it happened. Just like pawns, the pax and crew were taken captive for four months. (The cynical might question the convenient last-minute loading of a handful of silent yet military-looking men into Business class ex-London). I could of course be wrong about 9/11, but I feel there is nothing new that evil men create under the sun, in this world of little order.... Pass the cocoa – I'm ready for bed.

The new fleet

Day to day I was aware that there was something quite flawed about this new fleet. I remembered how my mate Mike, had warned me many years earlier that the airline was trying to set something up like this. We used to pass strikers who would stand at prominent points along the A23 dual carriageway at LGW with signs and placards. Our crew buses used to hoot them to offer our support, with the occasional leg out of the window for good measure. At that time you could not have envisaged, despite the apparent success of the campaign to demonstrate against proposed pay cuts and stricter working conditions, that within 12 years this supposedly archaic resolution would become a reality in a new LHR/LGW set up. It had only been dormant, like a hibernating grizzly, awaking to deliver its first snarl of the spring, and just like the wild animal, it had its own teething problems.

Even experienced crew members struggled within the first few months of inception to tame the beast that was 'the new fleet' and learn to play the game 'the BA way'.... I heard a similar story from so many juniors: "I love the job, but I can't afford to live." I was finding the same just trying to keep on top of my normal bills, month by month. One of my fellow cabin managers (another former chef) said to me that as he had been allocated training duties, he had lost out on £500 worth of flight duty pay per month which was a real source of anxiety for him. He said, "Where I was working before, trainers were really respected for their work, and rewarded financially. Here we are not, and I'm expected to deliver new-entrant courses which require me to work in my own time, often at weekends and late into the night. I'm exhausted and I don't have a life any more...". It seemed to me that the only way to make it work was to play the game until you could no longer play, and then leave, which is what happened to many: a steady trickle, which was absorbed into the high turnover rate allowed for by the airline. One out, maybe 500 waiting to come in.

There was a system in place where you could withdraw your flight duty pay through Travelex counters at the crew centre, up to a maximum of £300 per month. I relied on this cash to top up my bank account for standing orders, but one month I had gone over by about £50, which cued an automatic letter from my business manager (IBM). I was infuriated as I reread the hollow lines with the admonishment that I was "now no longer entitled to withdraw flight pay in advance of (my) salary date." I started to compose a retaliatory letter in my mind, but after an hour I calmed down and realised that this was a guy only doing his job, issuing corporate blanket-decisions from higher up.

As if that wasn't bad enough, there was a distinct tension between fleets which *seemed* to have been encouraged by senior management to keep everyone on their toes. As various crews came on/off, you could find yourself greeted – or deliberately ignored – by those belonging to different fleets, but hired by the same employer. I would spy crew-union bag tags with indicating those unhappiest with their lots. Others would try their best to make you feel small or intimidated by their derogatory comments, whereas others still were happy enough just to get on with you, or find out more about what it was like work for a fleet that was so closely scrutinised. Contrast that with the robotic nature of some of the CSMs I heard about, who would each major on a particular aspect of the job. Some would become 'champions' of uniform standards, and have an unhealthy obsession with the length of someone's skirt or their shade of lipstick. Others would hover over junior crew as they set up Club World meal trays, reducing them to nervous wrecks if the positioning of the crockery was not absolutely accurate. Still others, were ready to quash any attempt to of question the legitimacy of some fleet decisions. The pattern was to promote the high standards of the fleet, with the emotionless demeanour of an executioner at his work. What I saw was the attempt by many to feather their own nests for future careers that might not even exist, except for a few special chosen ones. (And I have since observed similar behaviour in other organisations.)

Caught between two worlds

I tried to be different, by retaining my identity while loosely playing by the rules. One girl told me half-an-hour into a long haul flight that she had just told several of her colleagues: "You don't know how lucky you are to have him as our CSM." They also gathered around me in the galley, saying I reminded them of someone. It wasn't the first time, so I produced the magazine picture of Colin Firth from my file, to their gasps: "Oh yeah!" came back in unison. (I think it was probably more of a gasp at why on earth someone would carry around a picture of the aforementioned actor in their work folder.) Still, I had the same from an old man boarding at DEN the following evening. As I took his C-boarding pass greeting him: "Good evening Mr...", he stopped, turned around and called down to his wife 20m behind him on the jetty: "Hey Marge! It's Colin Firth!" (He turned out to be quite a character – an 85-year-old ex-US Navy pilot.) You see, there must have been something in it, so I hung on therefore to that picture. It saved time when people said I reminded them of someone, and it gave me a sense of identity.

Day to day, I just carried on reluctantly as I thought about my wife and young family back home, needing my presence. But I was caught between two worlds: I was committed to a job to pay the bills and all the money I owed, but I felt alone, in a no-man's land and, privately, my own mental health was on a knife edge. We men should really take our stresses seriously. Middle aged men run the highest risk of suicide. I barely confided in anyone, but sometimes I would lean against the door at 1L on the take-off run, and wonder what it might be like to operate the handle at the point of aircraft rotation and jump out. Thankfully, that remained a day dream and I carried on working for the airlines until I could finally do it no longer. I handed in my notice to my manager and breathed a sigh of relief. I was going home, but to quite what I didn't know....

Return to base – for the final time

My final long-haul – yet another DEN – was quiet, but the most memorable part was to be sat in the flight-deck for the landing back at base. The five-mile approach to runway 09 Left LHR on a sunny day, is unsurpassed in taking in the beauty of the English landscape. The aircraft banked left and right in order to eventually hit the localiser (ILS radio guidance) and then fully establish for a final approach, passing directly over the battlements of Windsor Castle. All around, inbound airliners glided above and below, and just being in the front allowed me the best panorama of all. It always amazed me how gently the largest aircraft seemed to land, as if on velvet. Trevor, a van driver, once told me it was because they had 'a triple-bogey' landing gear (aka undercarriage or simply main wheels). A triple-bogey always made me smile as it reminded me of my school days. Sitting high up in the 777 front-end, I thought of being in the Tristar when I had started my journey all those years ago. The 777, however, was not held together by gaffer tape, goodwill or Reg's metre-long screwdriver.

It amused me that on one of my last short-haul duties before abandoning the airline industry for good, I was part of a trio on a three-day trip to Paris and Vienna, where each of us had been mistaken for a famous actor/actress. The unlikely trio consisted of Ben Stiller, Uma Thurman and Colin Firth. As we walked through those airports I wondered if anyone else could see the likenesses.... I cracked open the Champagne on the way to the Viennese hotel in the Mercedes Vito minibus, and handed around the plastic cups to the other five grateful recipients. The upside of the job. Cheers!

My absolutely final flight was a late-afternoon MAN on an ex-BMI (British Midland) A319. Twenty-seven pax out, and just one on the return, so doubtful the flight made even the fuel costs back. I remember the F/O had positioned his seat ultra-low on the tracks so that he resembled a boy racer. I was amazed he could see out of the window. The Italian hostie working with me up front couldn't believe I shared the same continental roots: "There is nothing Italian about-a-you!" she announced in the crew bus. I slowly and methodically retaliated, "Wow, look at your hair with it's blonde streaks – so blonde and yet, so typically Italian....." "Ah, shadduppa!" she responded. On the return, she was the one who bundled a load of mixed miniatures into a bag for me, as her leaving present to me on behalf of the unwitting airline, in time-honoured tradition. Not so bad after all....

I slept the night at that dark room in the airport for one final time, ready to surrender my goods the following morning. I had stuck with this job for about 18 months before finally turning in my uniform, bar keys and manuals. Capt. Maunder – whose tea-covered radios I had mopped up years earlier – happened to be in the office when I handed in my uniform. He looked at me with a mixture of sadness and incredulousness, as it was the sort of airline you don't leave. In fact when you see how many cabin crew there are on the other fleets who don't even make my equivalent rank, you'll see just how many have been there for 25 years or longer, at the same level. The beauty of old contracts and unlimited 'box-payment' expenses claims. There was of course a chasm of around £100,000 between the aforementioned captain and myself. The questionable beauty of 'new fleet' contracts and our capped expense claims. No more free hotel stationery, commuting at odd hours or company-issue iPad. Even with all this, I still had a sense of pride in having worked for the national flag-carrier, but it was time to draw a line underneath it.

I had a souvenir which I had acquired from a heap of scrap: an A320 flight-deck window, I don't know why I took it, but it brought me some closure. I retired to my faithful little red diesel Fiesta, which had been my transport for the past 18 months, and soon hit the road homewards. The car had an extra 35,000 miles on the clock and had served me well, costing me £20 in fuel for a

200-mile round-trip every time. Slinging my crew-bags into the boot for the final time, I paused for a couple of minutes to watch a handful of landings on the adjacent LHR runway, before driving home. You know when it's the end of one season and the start of another. Taking the leap has become easier and easier for me to do, but I still get a nervous feeling in my stomach every time I do it. I had cashed in my meagre pension and paid for a few days away in a static caravan on the Isle of Wight, during which I had the best chase-games with my kids ever, right next to the sea, beside a field of llamas, a buffalo and some chickens. The adrenaline was better than any take-off I had ever experienced. Most other crew would have gone to Dubai to stay at a five-star, but I couldn't stretch to that with six of us, plus I would have missed out on the animals. The whole LHR experience had been an education, during which I had also managed to educate myself, leading to an eventual law degree on the side. I could now add the meaningful letters LLB after my name if I wanted to, instead of others adding rude names.

Chapter Ten

Reverse thrust: leaving the airline world...

"The flying never leaves your blood" according to Tony H....So, where did this leave the reluctant air-steward, once he had left the industry for good?

He dressed as a storm-trooper. (https://www.youtube.com/watch?v=NikCW-xG4gM) Or you can simply type in "Visor DJ scum" .He started his own business teaching drums. He became a cycling instructor, encouraging both young and old, and delighted in giving people confidence on the roads – that way he could wear shorts all year round. He taught pre-school children how to sing, by using teddy bears and rubber pigs as props: it was a better rate of pay than driving Transit vans. He thought he had heard 'the calling', but decided he didn't suit a dog collar, so continues to be the drummer at church. He joined a housing association, and became an advocate to the vulnerable and the voiceless. He studied law as a post-grad and tried to become a solicitor, but found all avenues blocked. (A 2:2 in Law gets you nowhere.) He joined a local authority in strategic asset-planning for housing developments. He wears hearing aids when no one is looking. He now has teenagers, which makes him feel older. In fact, he *is* older and his hair is substantially greyer. His wife is also older, which makes him feel a little better. He started to write books – it's just an experiment. He still struggles with making sense of his identity, but has settled for the fact that he may be an enigma. And, when he hangs up laundry on the washing line outside, he still smiles when he sees a four engined aircraft shooting its vapour trails across the morning sunrise sky, imagining its journey across the Atlantic, and what must be happening in the cabin in those moments. So, to wind up this story, here's a selection of random facts learned from my time in the airline industry, and one or two more recent ones....

- Every time there's a crash, the industry learns from it and applies preventative measures. For example, the 1985 Manchester British Airtours flight 28M 737 fire: since then, the fire-training alone is vastly improved for BCF (fire extinguisher) deployment, the wearing of crew smoke hoods and evacuation procedures.

- Pilots and cabin crew have just 90 seconds in which to evacuate a burning airliner, and escapees should then be guided away from an aircraft, upwind of the fire.

- The average life expectancy of a UK airline is about ten years. (Ask Byron, one of my fellow dispatchers: he worked for three airlines that went bust in succession. I'd say he was jinxed rather than informed.) Zoom lasted six years while XL went down after 14 years having absorbed other brands along the way such as JMC. There is a constant trend for merging and rebranding. Monarch did very well, then, to last from 1968 to 2017.

- If a chartered airliner makes 'a go-around' (aborted landing) on finals (final approach) because the cabin crew haven't secured the cabin in time, then all the profits that flight would have made, are obliterated by the extra fuel consumed. It happened to a whole fledgling crew I knew.

- Dave the rockabilly marshaller at BRS, once told me that there's a higher than usual proportion of winter/spring flights returning with coffins on board from the Canary Islands, as if the elderly decide to go out one last time....

- Northwest DC10's used to smell of coffee, Randy Mills, my fellow straight air steward used to tell me. He should know, as he used to shuttle all sorts of buggy pax around LGW, to many different airliners. Randy said the funniest-looking crew belonged to Alitalia and Olympic: male SCCMs used to wear caps that made them look like *carabinieri.*

- If you're ever feeling bored, or have ages to go until pay-day, like the other *SAS's* I used to hang out with, then you could do worse than take the LGW North/South Terminal mono-rail backwards and forwards for an hour. It's free, lasts for about two minutes, and you'll receive the feeling that you've been somewhere for an evening, even though it starts to feel very familiar after the first return journey. It's either that or light a fire in the woods, and wonder what your life will look like in ten years time....

- JTR, Greece was "a captain-only approach" due to the 'out-to-sea and sharp turn', combined with the precision needed to land on the short (2,125m) civil/military runway said a Thomson pilot, now at BA.

• If you overshoot the 2,500m runway 10 at FAO (Faro, Portugal) you'll end up in the sea, specifically the North Atlantic Ocean.

• DEN (Denver, Colorado) does almost certainly have a secret subterranean military command centre, which explains the inordinate number of runways built there. Why else? It's not exactly busy like ORD (Chicago O'Hare). DEN is certainly the strangest airport to wander through, not only because of the mystical Native American music piped through speakers constantly. Having been there half a dozen times, I generally concur with the theories that it is a front for something far more sinister and secretive, symbolised by the blue horse sculpture with the evil-looking red eyes as you leave/enter the airport. It fell on its' sculptor and killed him. Enough said?

• T-tailed airliners such as the MD88 and the Fokker 100 have lower stalling speeds owing to their wing roots being further towards the rear to balance the planes' COGs (centre of gravity). Pilots have stall-warning systems in all flight decks. The horn activates if the plane senses the speed is too low, so the most appropriate action is to drop the nose or increase the throttles: ignore the horn and you drop out of the sky.

• Taxi fuel (the amount burned from engine start to entering the runway) is about 200kg for a Dash 8. Multiply that by up to eight times for a 747....

- A rudder section for an ATR turboprop costs about £95,000. When you need a spare, you pay the price.

- It is possible to climb up the instrument landing system (ILS) pylons at LGW to take selfies, but if caught you'll be arrested and probably be beaten, tied up and shipped to Guatemala. (Okay, I made that last bit up.)

- Middle Eastern carriers like Etihad, Emirates and Qatar have funds pumped into them, as sheiks love to outdo each other. Airlines: every sheikh should have one.

- Therapeutic Oxygen needed in the cabin? Action for cabin crew: turn the oxygen on via a request to the flight-deck, then, back in the cabin, plug the mask in. Should you get this in the wrong order, all the masks in the cabin will drop down and create a panic on the scale of Pompeii.

- Taking of oxygen, don't carry unregulated items in the hold. Why? See the cause of the Valujet DC-9 crash in 1996. The therapeutic oxygen the DC-9 was carrying was in breach of carriage rules. A fire ignited and exploded all the bottles. The dispatcher should not have signed that one to go. Sounds like the sort of thing I would probably have allowed....

- Pilots wear EROS (Emergency Response Oxygen System) masks in the event of a decompression. Squeeze to activate from an outboard console, pass the contraption over your head and you then resemble an oversized rodent, but at least you're still breathing....

- Don't fly with a cold: Even at the expense of my sinuses, I was never one to miss out on a duty and the promise of a croissant with a mini-marmalade.

- My mum and dad would have cried at the sight of every part-used bottle of red, white and Champagne being unceremoniously poured down the toilets in preparation for landing at LHR after a long-haul flight. It's an HM Customs requirement, and to simply re-cork a bottle or two and pop them in your bag to drink at home would have resulted in instant dismissal, if caught. Still, pouring expensive Champagne down the U-bend never felt right to me.

- It's ok for a guy to moisturise, and to drink tomato juice during a flight, as it's good for the skin. Not so great to wear eyeliner unless there's a valid reason, such as you happen to be Green Day about to go onstage at Glastonbury. Guys, it's really for the girls on board, not the boys – you know who you are....

- MH370, the 'missing 777' on the morning of its disappearance, according to nearby witnesses on an island in the Indian Ocean, was apparently spotted flying so low, that it was possible to make out the Malaysian logo and even its doors, heading in the direction of a 'secret' US military base. That military base on Diego Garcia happens to be the equivalent of Guantanamo Bay, Cuba, and is used for 'detainment and interrogation'. If this is remotely true, then there could have been something or someone on board the airliner that was of great importance to US

Intelligence services....like an 80kg gyroscope, and maybe some Chinese scientists. Ahem.

- Boeing's 737 *New Generation* and the 737 *Max* may sound like Prince's backing band or a fizzy drink, but they have sadly had a bumpy ride. At the time of writing, the 737 Max has been grounded owing to two fatal accidents caused by an Airbus-style system glitch where seemingly the plane knows better than its master, by lowering the nose without pilot action when the plane encounters high angles of attack....

- Concorde: what happened? For the first time in airline history, we are not making new ground in terms of speed across the continents. There was something magical and exciting about hearing something fast going overhead, and espying the distinctive white dart cross the skies. I was on Clifton Suspension Bridge, Bristol, for its final homecoming flight to Filton in 2003 and, as it dipped its wings, I saluted. (In the photo, I'm stood next to the bright orange coat in the middle of the bridge.) We even sang, *'There'll always be an England....'*

Epilogue

'Line up and wait…'.

That's the phrase I used to love hearing on my bulky air-band radio, listening into flight/ATC communications as I leaned over the railings of the visitor centre at LGW. The radio sequence could sound something like this: *"Speedbird 2286 Alpha, after the next landing – a company 757 – line up and wait runway 26 Left."* The pilot, as per international radio procedures, would echo back the instructions to acknowledge. If I was ever lucky enough to be in the flight deck for take-off, especially as a junior, then I would be party to all those conversations and the banter in the front seats. It is a signal that all the preparations are complete, and you are ready for the departure: await the call ("cleared for take-off"), set the throttles and then let the brakes go….

I used to watch these aircraft from all over the world come and go, marvelling at the big ones like cargo DC10s ('affectionately' known as 'Death Cruisers'), shiny bare-metal American Airlines MD-11s or BA 747s as they lumbered carefully down 2-6- Left, engines whining and gathering speed, using up nearly the whole of the two-mile length of the runway if they were fully-laden, before rotating gracefully into the air. Ironically, it was two of the smallest aircraft types with Sixties and Seventies' engine technology, that used to make the loudest noise by far at Gatwick Airport. Boeing 737-200s and BAC 1-11s with their cigar-shaped turbofan engines, used to crackle and roar as they sped down the runway, literally shaking the ground, before they climbed away, emitting two polluting streams of black smoke into the skies, just for good measure.

To 'line up and wait' therefore is to be in a state of readiness for flight. It is the end result of behind-the-scenes preparation, maybe a year in advance from all sorts of teams, which includes technicians, sales agents, engineers, cargo departments, forecasters and strategic planners. The flight, therefore, is the culmination of all the work that has gone on beforehand. I have an old blurred photo of me standing next to an L1011 nose wheel, and I am truly dwarfed. This makes sense of the fact that the component parts of what allows a flight to get up in the air, completely overshadow the in-flight element, yet that is the part that people see and recall. If you had a good experience overall in the air, then you would almost certainly want to fly with that carrier again. What you don't see is the backstage work that has allowed the C/As and the flight crew to take the glory.

I am thankful for the fact that I am still here, having amassed somewhere in the region of 2,000 flight sectors, with the only physical harm being a scald (severe burn caused by boiling water) in LUX (Luxembourg). The caterer managed to drop an urn with near-boiling water (88 degrees Celcius) straight over my head, while I was checking trolley contents. It was so hot, that it actually felt freezing. The paramedics were called to the plane and treated me with ice packs. (I would have settled for a KitKat Chunky as a treat, but they didn't have any.) I decided to operate the flight back with minimal delay, and a doctor in C-class examined my scalp for burn damage.

Oh, and I had a near miss with a taxi-ing 737-500 on the same airfield one Sunday afternoon. We were on a long turnaround, so I sat on an embankment listening to music. Very little was happening at the airfield until the arrival of the 737 which I watched, wondering which taxiways it would follow to get to the apron. It was the sudden realisation at the last minute that it was coming towards me. How the two Lux-air pilots chuckled visibly, waving, as they saw me run up the bank to avoid the port wing, which would have taken my head off as it passed at 30 mph taxi speed. Never mind that – I nearly lost my Walkman.

My mum bought me a black beanie hat years ago, from Brighton. It had a green leaf and capital letters in red declaring 'HIGH LIFE'. I explained to her that it was a dirty great cannabis leaf, and she appeared dismayed for a moment: "Oh, I saw 'High Life' and thought it described you – as an air steward…". I smiled gratefully. Then, obviously cogitating, she became more animated and declared: "Prince Charles wants to legalise it – it's very controversial!" I miss my mum. I've also mislaid that hat.

I cry when I hear the ATC transcripts of Concorde's last departure from JFK in 2003. It must be the knowledge that I was a part of it, being a fan, an ex-employee and a guest on that famous white dart which touched so many hearts worldwide.

I've lost touch with pretty much everyone I used to work with apart from Demetrius, Renald, and Phil from BRS. I have an idea of who might be still flying and who might not, but I do know that all of us have grown up into lives with responsibilities, be they kids, mortgages, proper jobs and in many cases, stable relationships.

When I set about writing this book, it seemed to gush out. I guess I write to make sense of those few years, the in-betweens and the post-airline era. I don't know whether you work in the industry, are thinking of joining it, or simply wanted to find out a little more about what goes on in this rarefied world...? If I've put you off joining the industry, then I'm sorry. If I've encouraged you to join, then I'm still sorry. If you're a regular flyer and knew about all this stuff, then congratulations – you know too much.

I sent a sample chapter off to a chartered surveyor friend who said: "Prune the use of 'I': at the moment it reminds me of the *Readers Digest* stories that my old dad used to read on the Gary Glitter – nuts to facts – write what makes you laugh...!" The first draft was sent to a local publisher who said to me: "Use 'I' – the minute you start saying 'you', you've lost the reader...". Another author who is a best-seller, loved my anecdotes and advised me what to ditch. You know what? I aimed in the middle, just like my school-friend with the bad eyesight who was cycling towards two juggernauts. Anyway, if it's killed an otherwise boring hour in a faceless airport lounge, then I'm glad for you. If I've offended you, I'm sorry, but it'll only hurt for a minute, then you can chalk it up to experience. As you begin your own take-off roll, things will be racing through your mind. I hope my stories have done what they said they might – entertain and maybe even inspire you? Don't feel you have to answer that – I'm sensitive. Maybe you've read this and you're thinking "What a load of...." That's ok. Maybe your book will be ten times better.

"Ladies and gentlemen, as you can see the captain has now switched on the 'Fasten seat belt' signs, indicating our final approach. Please therefore return to your seat and make sure your seatbelt is securely fastened. The toilets are no longer in use. Please make a note of your nearest usable exits. I hope you've enjoyed your flight with me, and I look forward to welcoming you back on board in the near future. Cabin crew – seats for landing."

For now, the Reluctant Air Steward will go quiet. Always watch the quiet ones....

THE END (Maybe....)